Edgar Evans - Extempore

By Robert Little

Little
press & public relations

Acknowledgements

I am grateful for Edgar Evans' contributions to the researching of this book and for him allowing me access to his photographic files and memorabilia. I am grateful, too, for the advice and guidance I have received from Gina Boaks at the Royal Opera House, and for the various contributions to this book which have come from Janet Chivers, LA (Lewis) Davies, Brian Godfrey, Martin Hill, John Howells, Peter Jenkin, Lynne Lewis, John Quinn, Hilary Tangye, and Len Williams.

I am also grateful to have been able to quote from the following books:

- 'Opera Biographies' (published by Werner Laurie, 1955)
- 'Mr Showbusiness, the autobiography of Vic Oliver' (published by George G Harrap & Co Ltd, 1954)
- 'Erich Kleiber, a Memoir by John Russell (published by Andre Deutsch, 1957)
- 'The Quiet Showman', the biography of David Webster by Montague Haltrecht (published by Collins, 1975)
- 'A Knight at the Opera' by Sir Geraint Evans (published by Michael Joseph, July 1984),

along with several newspapers' and periodicals' comments on Edgar Evans and his achievements.

Edgar Evans would also like to publicly record his grateful thanks to the Rev Goronwy Evans, a Unitarian minister in Cardiganshire, who has championed Edgar Evans' career over many years, writing about him in newspapers, magazines and books and also arranging for Edgar to feature in radio and television programmes.

Robert Little, St Albans, November 2005

Published by Bob Little Press & PR, 23 Sherwood Avenue, St Albans, Herts, AL4 9QJ

ISBN 0-9543113-1-0

Cover design by S&W Design, St Albans, Hertfordshire
Typeset by PJC Design Ltd, Northampton
Printed and bound by Newman Thomson, Burgess Hill, West Sussex

Other books from Bob Little Press & PR include The Canvas Chapel, ISBN 0-9543113-0-2.

Dedication from Edgar Evans:

To Nan and Huw – and to my mother, Margaret, who believed in me vocally and encouraged me to go on.

Foreword

There was a time when one of London's most exclusive clubs was to be found in a vast cellar in Covent Garden. This was the canteen of the Royal Opera House, located directly beneath the orchestra stalls. Here was the daily meeting place of a crowd of singers, dancers, orchestral players, extras and backstage staff. It was noisy (especially when opera singers were on call) and it was jolly. And it was almost certainly here, at a tableful of principal singers, that I would have met Edgar Evans, when I first came to Covent Garden.

At that time there was still a true resident opera company at the Garden. Whereas nowadays there is but a constantly changing procession of principal guest artists, in 1962 and for a few years to come, there were some 40 principal singers on full-time contract. There were veterans like Edith Coates, Geraint Evans, John Lanigan and Otakar Kraus; artists at the peak of their career like Amy Shuard, Marie Collier, Josephine Veasey, Joan Carlyle, John Shaw, Kenneth Macdonald, Michael Langdon, Forbes Robinson, Joseph Rouleau and David Ward, and newcomers with everything to play for like Gwyneth Jones, Elizabeth Vaughan, Peter Glossop and (a little later) Margaret Price. Distinguished among the veterans was Edgar Evans.

In fact, Edgar was a member of the legendary team which was recruited in 1946 by David Webster and Karl Rankl to be the nucleus of the post-war opera company. Everything had to be built up from scratch, as the Opera House had, ignominiously, been serving as a dance hall throughout the war years. The Sadler's Wells Ballet (now The Royal Ballet) kept the curtain up for several months while their opera colleagues were getting their act together. The fledgling opera company eventually made its debut in Purcell's Fairy Queen, with Edgar in the cast.

By the 1960s the company had taken wing in a big way. Under the dynamic leadership of its music director, George Solti, it had won a place of honour among the top half dozen companies of the world.

I associate Edgar very much with the euphoria and cameraderie of this golden period. As I write, he is well into his 90s and I believe that he is the sole survivor among the principals of the original Covent Garden Opera Company. There were heroes in those days and we are now privileged to share the recollections of one of the best of them.

Keith Grant
General Manager of the Royal Opera Company
and of the English Opera Group from 1962 to 1973

Introduction

It was with some trepidation that I approached The Royal College of Music one Wednesday evening in early October 1976.

For many years – since I was eight years old or so - I had enjoyed singing and had hoped that, once my voice had broken, I would be a tenor like my father. Moreover, ever since, as a 17 and 18 year old, I had sung a few solos in school concerts, I had wanted to have my voice trained so that I could be a professional singer.

As an economics undergraduate at University College, Cardiff, I had enrolled at the Welsh College of Music and Drama as a part time student. There, I studied with Gerald Davies who, so I understood, had, in his time, sung at Covent Garden and Sadler's Wells. In fact, Gerald Davies had sung the small part of Goro in 'Madam Butterfly' at Covent Garden in 1937, Later, he became a principal tenor at Sadler's Wells.

Gerald Davies did his best for me but, when my university studies ended in the summer of 1976 and I got a job in Wembley Park, in north London, I asked him to recommend a singing teacher for me in the London area. Unhesitatingly he recommended Edgar Evans – then recently retired as a principal tenor with the Royal Opera and currently teaching at the Royal College of Music in South Kensington.

I contacted Edgar and he asked me to come and sing for him at the College one evening, at the end of his 'teaching day'.

I was extremely nervous as I made my way into the College and up the stairs to his studio. I knocked on the door and, as bidden, entered.

I seemed to me to be a large room, containing a grand piano and a fairly grand man. Knowing Edgar to be – as Gerald Davies had called him – 'a real Welshman', I hoped to impress him by speaking in my very best (but not very fluent) Welsh.

After a few faltering exchanges – my Welsh wasn't up to the demands being made of it and Edgar could make neither head nor tail of what I was trying to tell him – he said: "Speak English."

I didn't mind that. What I did mind was having to sing for him.

Edgar accompanied me on the piano – playing chords rather than all the notes, while listening intently to the sounds I was making.

I sang 'Caro Mio Ben', by Giordano. It was obvious I was ill at ease.

"Don't be nervous!" Edgar exclaimed. "Just try your best. All of us can only ever do our best."

Not only was it good advice but it broke the ice and did the trick. I sang again. It was better but, even so, Edgar didn't seem as impressed as I had originally hoped.

"I'll give you six lessons," he said. "If you can't sing 'over' (the technique required for tenors to sing above an F) by the end of the sixth lesson, we'll call it a day. OK?"

I agreed. After all, he had agreed to teach me – albeit for a probationary period of six weekly lessons.

Thankfully, Edgar couldn't count. At the end of the sixth lesson, when I was still having some difficulty understanding the singing technique he was trying to give me, he said: "Do you want to come again next week?"

"Yes," I said.

That reply set the seal on a growing friendship that has lasted from that day to this.

I never did achieve my ambition of becoming a professional singer – although, with the vocal technique I culled from Edgar's teaching, I did a lot of amateur and semi-professional singing and even gave two (unsuccessful) auditions for the Royal Opera in the very early 1990s. However, Edgar's teaching has brought me a deeper appreciation of vocal technique in singing, while the friendship of Edgar and his wife, Nan, brought pleasure to my whole family over the years.

When my wife, Helen, and I were married – on Saturday 18th October 1980 – we asked Edgar to sing for us at the ceremony (while we went to sign the register). He protested that he had retired from singing in public – but, with characteristic generosity, agreed to sing.

His performance – of 'Ombra mai fu', otherwise known as the famous 'Largo' from Handel's opera, Xerxes – was not only beautifully phrased and highly impressive but probably his last public performance on any stage.

As our professional relationship developed, it was easier for me – working in Wembley Park - to visit Edgar at his house in nearby Harrow, rather than go to the Royal College of Music.

Most of the time I brought him songs and operatic roles that were unknown to him in his professional career. They included sentimental

Victorian ballads and Gilbert & Sullivan tenor roles. But, to each one, Edgar brought a thorough professionalism and a steely determination to teach me how best to convey the emotions of both the words and music.

Mine was not the only voice that he coaxed to achieve more than might otherwise have been expected of it. Many of his former pupils have made careers as professional singers in the UK and throughout Europe. These include Andrew Yates, Glyn McKay, Jane Kamargue, Marie Miller, David Rose, Bryan Secombe, a former principal singer with the D'Oyly Carte Opera Company before joining the Royal Opera; Gary Sutcliffe, who is with the English National Opera, and Philip Salmon, a tenor who has built an international reputation as a soloist.

Yet this is not their story. It is his.

In many ways, Edgar Evans' story is remarkable, containing any number of unexpected twists and turns.

It is a far cry from being born and brought up on a farm in Cardiganshire in West Wales before the First World War to becoming a principal tenor at the Royal Opera in Covent Garden immediately after the Second World War and on into the pre-Thatcherite world of the 1970s.

As in every career, chance meetings played their part. And, as in every successful career, so did a great deal of hard work – not all of it aimed specifically in the direction of music.

This is Edgar Evans' story as, principally, he told to it me over a number of visits to his house in Harrow in the early months of 2005. At the time, he was 92 years old and his memory was as bright and sharp as it had ever been when applied to learning an operatic role or, in earlier days, learning a new milk round while working for the Royal Arsenal Co-Operative Society.

Although it is Edgar's story, told in his own words from chapter two onwards, 'reported speech marks' are only used in this book to denote passages of dialogue - for the sake of easier reading and understanding.

I hope that you enjoy reading this book as much as I have enjoyed researching and writing it. I hope it offers some valuable insights not only into the psyche of the last surviving principal of the re-formed Royal Opera company in 1946 but also into the people and their ways of life – both musical and otherwise – of the inter-war years, the years of the Second World War and the post-war era.

Robert Little
November 2005

Contents

Foreword – by Keith Grant, former manager of the Royal Opera Company   iv

Introduction – by Robert Little   v

Chapter one: Edgar Evans: in a nutshell   1

Chapter two: To begin at the ending   6

Chapter three: Opera and opportunities   8

Chapter four: Cwrt Newydd and Caruso   11

Chapter five: School, singing – and snogging on the organ stool   17

Chapter six: Counting chickens   22

Chapter seven: Impromptu impressions   24

Chapter eight: Further and Freer   27

Chapter nine: Milk with music   30

Chapter ten: War work   36

Chapter eleven: Chance and a cigarette packet   45

Chapter twelve: Dyslexia and Dancairo   49

Chapter thirteen: Nerves and a nag   51

Chapter fourteen: Grimes and gaffes   60

Chapter fifteen: Dr Sargent and Mr Evans   64

Chapter sixteen: Crits and compliments   68

Chapter seventeen: Teachers and Turandot   74

Chapter eighteen: Royal reminiscences   78

Chapter nineteen: Anecdotes and animosities   82

Chapter twenty: Gellhorn and Hermann   92

Chapter twenty one: Miscellany   100

Appendix one: Press notices   112

Appendix two: Workload   118

Appendix three: The official story   144

Appendix four: The art of singing   148

Appendix five: The Edgar Evans file - some key documents   153

Appendix six: Nan Evans (nee Walters), 1910 - 1998   163

List of illustrations   168

Index   171

Chapter one

Edgar Evans: in a nutshell

Edgar Evans will be best remembered for creating the role of
Hermann in Tchaikovsky's The Queen of Spades at the Royal
Opera House, Covent Garden.

In all, he sang some 45 roles – most of them major ones - at Covent
Garden from 1946 - when, as one of its three principal tenors, he
became a founder member of the Covent Garden Opera Company - to
his retirement in 1975. In that time, he sang more roles and more
performances at the Opera House than any other artist.

Those roles included Steva in the first British stage performance of
Jenufa, Zinovy in the British premiere of Katerina Ismailova, the
Interpreter and A Celestial Messenger in the premiere of Vaughan
Williams' Pilgrim's Progress, Andres in the first Covent Garden
Wozzeck and Captain Davidson in Richard Rodney Bennett's Victory. In
addition, he was Dmitri in the company's first Boris Godunov, Hermann
in the first Covent Garden Queen of Spades under Kleiber, Riccardo
(Gustavus) in the first Masked Ball performed at Covent Garden since
the War, Aegisth in the first post-War Elektra, Hellenus in The Trojans
conducted by Kubelik, Narraboth in the Brook-Dali Salome, and Froh
in the first post-War Covent Garden Ring.

Born in Cardiganshire in 1912, the son of Margaret and William
Evans, a farmer, and the youngest - by eight years - of 13 children,

1

Edgar heard the voice of Enrico Caruso over the radio at the age of eight. From then on his only and all-embracing ambition was to be a singer, despite his father's ambitions for him to become a banker or an architect.

Completely untaught, Edgar practised both 'preaching' in the declamatory 'Welsh chapel' style and singing in a barn-cum-boilerhouse on the farm. As a boy, he was always being told that he sang too loudly. Only his mother encouraged him to sing by saying that his voice had a 'ring' to it unlike those of the rest of his family – and, indeed, anyone else in his home community in Cwrt Newydd, Cardiganshire.

Having failed dismally as a singer in the local Eisteddfod when aged 11, Edgar – then aged 17 - improved enough to steal the show at an end of term concert at his secondary school in Newquay, Cardiganshire. He went on to win various prizes at local Eisteddfodau as a baritone.

The opportunity to take up singing professionally came when this, by now, articled pupil to the County Architect was heard singing 'Loch Lomond' in a pub, called The Irish House, Piccadilly, while on a rugby trip to London in 1935. The 'talent scout' took him by taxi to The Odd Spot nightclub in London's West End, from where he was referred to Arthur Fagg, conductor of The London Choral Society, who knew Dawson Freer, a singing teacher at the Royal College of Music.

One week later, Edgar became a pupil of Freer's - who began by telling him that he sang too loudly! These early lessons helped Edgar to establish himself as a professional singer, but he felt that his voice and vocal technique improved immeasurably when, later in his career, the Royal Opera arranged for him to continue his studies - this time (in 1950) with the Italian maestro Luigi Ricci in Rome.

For 18 months, Edgar studied with Dawson Freer, using up his legacy from his father – who had died in 1927 – to support himself and pay the six guineas for every ten singing lessons. Running out of funds, Edgar took on a milk round in Camberwell – for the Royal Arsenal Co-Operative - getting up at five o'clock each morning and, eventually, progressed to the round in Cold Harbour Lane in Brixton – where the young John Major lived.

Some 18 months after meeting Freer, Edgar gave his first ever audition. As a result, Lilian Baylis offered Edgar a contract to sing as a chorister, under the direction of chorus master Geoffrey Corbett, with the Sadler's Wells Opera Company in 1937 on a salary of £3 a week.

That first contract from Sadler's Wells offered him the same wage as he was getting as a milkman. He never had any regrets about changing career.

He spent the War as a member of the Police Reserve – again on wages of £3 a week - having been turned down for service in the armed forces. All his life, he was dogged with kidney problems.

Throughout the War, he was singing in shows for CEMA and ENSA, entertaining the troops, under the direction of Walter Legge and performing with artists including Maggie Teyte, Joyce Grenfell, Richard Addinsell (composer of the Warsaw Concerto) and many others. After 18 months, he left the Police to concentrate on performing, and, in all, he sang in over 500 concerts during the war.

In the latter years of the war and when hostilities ceased, Edgar toured the main theatres in the UK and Europe, singing with The Anglo-Russian Merry Go Round Company performing in a number of cities, including Paris.

For a while, he was in Bernard Delfont's production of Gay Rosalinda at the Palace Theatre, in London, under the musical direction of Richard Tauber. He later worked for Delfont again in a show in Ryde, on the Isle of Wight.

A chance meeting with Henry Robinson, formerly stage manager at Sadler's Wells, resulted in Edgar applying for an audition with the newly formed Covent Garden Opera Company. Singing 'E lucevan le stelle' from Tosca and the Flower Song from Carmen, Edgar was chosen from scores of tenor hopefuls from around the world and progressed successfully through three auditions to receive the offer of a contract from the Administrator, David Webster, in the middle of August 1946.

His first roles were as the bird god and lover in Purcell's Faerie Queene in a cast that included Michael Hordern, Constance Shacklock, Margot Fonteyn and Moira Shearer. He made his Covent Garden debut, deputising for Heddle Nash, as the Chavelier des Grieux in Manon, under the direction of Reginald Goodall.

He became one of the first British singers to sing in opera abroad after the War when Erich Kleiber took him to sing in Wagner's Ring in Rome, with the Rome Opera. Later, he was the tenor soloist in Beethoven's Choral Symphony when Kleiber conducted the work at Covent Garden at a concert to help establish an artists' pension fund.

From that first appearance as the Chevalier des Grieux – on 25th March 1947 - to his farewell performance, as the butler in The Visit of the Old Lady, by von Einem, at Glyndebourne, Edgar Evans was a well respected member of the music world. His acting and vocal ability evoked comparison with the very best and elicited reviews such as:

'His voice has a pleasant timbre and is produced with ease. But the most notable thing about his performance was the fact that it realised perfectly the elegant as well as the sentimental character of the melodic line.' (The Daily Telegraph, April 1947, on his debut as des Grieux in Manon)

'As the cheerful but unfortunate King of Sweden (in Masked Ball), Edgar Evans follows in the line of some of the greatest tenors who have ever sung in opera, including Jean de Reske and Caruso.' (Education, November 27, 1953)

Of that production of Masked Ball in 1953 – singing with Tito Gobbi and the Dutch soprano, Gré Brouwenstijn - Edgar commented: "Hearing Gobbi reminded me of Ricci's teaching. It inspired me to sing the best I ever sang."

Within six weeks of returning from Ricci in Rome, the higher part of his vocal range now completely secure, Edgar sang Calaf in Turandot under the baton of Sir John Barbirolli. He regularly demonstrated his remarkable strength of voice by singing several major roles including Pinkerton (in Madam Butterfly), Don Jose (Carmen), Max (Der Freischutz) and Peter Grimes in the same week.

Eventually the stress of this punishing schedule caught up with him and he was forced to rest for 20 weeks. After this he never resumed the pre-eminence among principal tenors at Covent Garden that had been his.

Subsequently, he conducted his share of masterclasses and adjudicated at singing competitions. Even in his later years, he had a regular procession of singers all anxious to learn his secrets of vocal technique and his opinion of their vocal talents and abilities.

On his retirement from Covent Garden, Edgar was invited – by Sir David Willcocks – to join the teaching staff at the Royal College of Music. For ten years he taught vocal technique there and many singers can pay tribute to his masterly teaching.

He sang with leading singers; with leading orchestras, both in this country and on the Continent, and worked with leading conductors including Erich Kleiber, Karl Rankl, Sir Thomas Beecham, Sir John Barbirolli, Sir Malcolm Sargent, Sir Georg Solti, Otto Klemperer, Rudolf Kempe and Carlo Maria Giulini. Among those to whom he felt he owed a special debt of gratitude was Peter Gellhorn who, as a repetiteur and conductor at Covent Garden, taught Edgar the part of Hermann in 'The Queen of Spades' in the remarkably short time of just 14 hours.

He sang the title role in Peter Grimes and Captain Vere (Billy Budd) after Peter Pears had initally brought these characters to theatrical life. He sang Dmitri in Boris Gudonov – in English - under Clemens Krause and, later, in Russian (being taught the part by David Lloyd Jones and Oda Slobotskyia); Steva in Janacek's Jenufa under Kubelik; the Drum Major in Alban Berg's Wozzeck, under Kleiber; Calaf in Turandot under Barbirolli and many more roles. Barbirolli – and Kleiber – were among

● *Edgar Evans.*

Edgar's favourite conductors, closely followed by Kempe and Giulini.

Only the recording studio failed to do justice to Edgar's robust, romantic voice. Appearances as Melot in Wagner's Tristan und Isolde (HMV) under Furtwangler; Britten's Albert Herring (Decca), with the composer conducting; a recently re-issued recording of Verdi's Don Carlos, in which Edgar sings the role of Lerma, and his recording of Nessun Dorma from Turandot are all that remain to stir the memory.

Edgar married Nan (nee Walters, died December 1998) on 19th August 1939. They had one son, Huw, who died in June 1999. Edgar has two grandchildren: Rebecca and Edward.

Chapter two

To begin at the ending

Most people start their professional singing careers at Glyndebourne and finish them at the Royal Opera House. I did things the other way around. My last operatic role was in 'The Visit of the Old Lady', an opera by von Einem, at Glyndebourne in 1974. The opera was conducted by John Pritchard and produced by John Cox.

I had never sung at Glyndebourne before then – and, obviously, I never sang there subsequently. So 'The Visit of the Old Lady' was both my Glyndebourne debut and my swan song.

I'd never really wanted to go to sing at Glyndebourne because I was so busy singing – and covering – major parts at Covent Garden.

Like everyone connected with opera in the UK, I knew the Christie family who ran Glyndebourne. I had met the 'old man' (who founded the opera festival) once. He wined and dined me in order to persuade me to sing the Rake in 'The Rake's Progress' at Glyndebourne. However, at the time – 1953 - I had just agreed to go to Southern Rhodesia, singing Rudolfo in 'La Boheme' under the baton of Sir John Barbirolli, so I never sang the Rake at Glyndebourne – or anywhere else for that matter.

We did 11 performances in Bulawayo – and the performances were not far apart. However, one night we went on a safari. The dust that arose from our excursion into the countryside was so dreadful that it got on my throat and I had to cancel my next performance as Rudolfo. I just couldn't sing! However, I was back singing the role, two days later.

It was then that I discovered the benefit of taking a 'swig' from an oxygen cylinder before going on stage to sing.

Since Bulawayo is some way above sea level, there were fears that members of the ballet – who were touring with us – would need some help to cope with the 'altitude problems'. So oxygen cylinders were put at the sides of the stage for the performers – and were well used by the dancers.

This particular night, fearing that the dust may not have completely left my throat, I took a swig from the cylinder – and found that it was very much easier to sing! The effect of taking oxygen – especially before singing the third act of La Boheme, which involves a lot of singing for Rudolfo – was to invigorate me. My lungs felt completely rejuvenated for about an hour afterwards.

Oddly enough, I never thought of taking oxygen again to help me sing – although I know that some of the other singers in the touring party did continue the practice.

● *At a party in Bulawayo with (from left) Joan Sutherland, the hostess Geraint Evans and John Comber.* (photo by Janet Chivers)

Chapter three

Opera and opportunities

Every April members of the Royal Opera received a letter telling them whether they were staying with the company – or not. I was fortunate to be kept on for nearly 30 years but, for the last five or six years of my time there, I realised that the end would come one day.

Those early years of the 1970s were the end of an operatic era – with the emergence of new, younger tenors, such as Jon Vickers who took over the role of Don Jose (Carmen) from me at the Opera House, as well as James McCracken, Placido Domingo and Luciano Pavarotti – with whom I sang in 'Rigoletto'.

I sang the role of Borza in 'Rigoletto' when, early on in his career, Luciano Pavarotti sang the role of the Duke. Unfortunately, in those days, Pavarotti was not taken too seriously and it was some time before he returned to Covent Garden after this performance.

I never sang the role of the Duke at Covent Garden, although, in the summer of 1947, I went on tour with a group from Covent Garden – it was the chorus plus four principals: myself, Edith Coates, Blanche Turner and Tom Williams, with the composer John Gardner as our accompanist and Douglas Robinson as our conductor – and, among our repertoire was the famous quartet from 'Rigoletto'.

One day in 1975, the administrator at the Royal Opera, Sir John

Tooley, asked me to go to see him. He told me what I'd suspected for a little while. After 30 seasons, I would not be returning to the Opera House after the summer break.

"What will you do?" John Tooley asked.

A few years previously, I'd met Redvers Llewellyn at a party in the Crush Bar at the Opera House. I'd known Redvers ever since I'd been in the chorus at Sadler's Wells Opera before the war. Redvers had sung the part of Rigoletto at Sadler's Wells in 1937/38, before going to teach at University College Aberystwyth – part of the University of Wales – and then at the Royal College of Music.

At the party, Redvers had said: "Edgar, I'd like you take over from me as a voice teacher at the Royal College of Music when I retire."

Within two years of making this comment, Redvers Llewellyn was dead – and there was a vacancy for a professor at the Royal College of Music.

"I'd like to teach," I said to Sir John.

So Sir John telephoned Sir David Willcocks, at that time the director of the Royal College of Music, and Michael Gough Matthews, the assistant director – who succeeded Sir David as director of the College. Sir David then got in touch with me. Pretty soon, I went to the College and met Sir David, along with his Assistant Director, the College Bursar and the Chairman of the board at the College.

At the end of a short and not very probing or comprehensive interview, they said: "OK. You can start next week."

So I did – and stayed there for another ten years. Those years, spent teaching at the Royal College of Music, were very happy years indeed for me and included my being made an 'Hon RCM' in 1980. When they came to an end in 1986, Michael Gough Matthews – by then the director of the College – arranged a splendid 'farewell lunch' for Richard Popplewell and me, the two professors who were retiring that term. We also received an invitation to attend one of the Royal Garden Parties, at Buckingham Palace, that year. That, too, was an occasion that my wife, Nan, and I greatly enjoyed.

When I started teaching at the College, I had relatively few pupils – because most of Redvers' pupils had gone to other teachers by the time I arrived. I inherited only three pupils from Redvers but they must have told their friends at the College about my methods because

I soon found a steady stream of students knocking on my door and asking for vocal lessons.

One girl had been told by another professor of singing at the College that she was no good and would never make a singer. Yet, after two terms studying with me, the girl won the top prize at the College for her singing.

Among my pupils was another rising star, Helen Kucharek, who could easily have made a good career in singing. However, I believe that she did too much operatic work too soon – taking on major roles for such companies as Pavilion Opera.

These youngsters want to be singers and so they are tempted with the offers of major roles as soon as they leave music college. But they need to take time to toughen up vocally before attempting these roles. Instead of doing whole roles, they should only be doing scenes from the operas. The traditional way to become an opera singer is to build up both the voice and vocal stamina over a number of years – being careful not to over-reach yourself in terms of the roles you perform. It seems that the modern way is a sort of 'kill or cure'. While a few singers may rise to the top of the profession under this regime, many more will find their voices ruined and their career as a singer will be over prematurely.

Singing grand opera is not the same as singing Gilbert & Sullivan operettas. Grand opera calls for strength and stamina – and good nerves. All of these take time to develop and nurture.

Chapter four

Cwrt Newydd and Caruso

I was born – at 2pm on a Sunday (9th June 1912) - at Cwrt Farm, near the village of Cwrt Newydd in Cardiganshire. In view of my later career, it was an auspicious day because it was the day of a rehearsal for a huge Cymanfa Ganu (hymn singing festival) which the Unitarian community – in which I was brought up – held annually in our area. It was a sufficiently prestigious event for it to attract the top choral conductors from the South Wales valleys to lead it.

● *Cwrt Farm with Edgar's sister Maggie and brother Dai.*

11

[The Welsh Revival – or Diwygiad - of 1904 had had its effect on the part of Cardiganshire where Edgar was born and brought up. By the time Edgar was a approaching his teenage years, the chapels were still full with people who had experienced a spiritual awakening only some 15 to 20 years earlier.

Edgar tells two stories about the Diwygiad: one of a postman who, in the excitement of strange and inexplicable events prompted by this religious awakening, was convinced that he had heard angelic voices singing while he was on his rounds. The other story is a joke – which, perhaps, illustrates how the remarkable events of the Diwygiad had been accepted by the whole community and subsumed into the local culture by the 1920s.

The story is told that, during one of the revivalist meetings, one young lady – sitting in the gallery of the chapel – was overcome by the emotion of the event and fainted, falling over the balcony but, thankfully, becoming caught by one of the candelabra that lit the church. In the process, gravity had draped the young lady's skirt over her upside down body, revealing her underclothes.

Instantly, the preacher says: "The Lord will strike blind anyone who takes advantage by looking at that young lady!"

And one of the men in the body of the congregation turns to his companion and says: "I think I'll risk one eye..."]

I was the youngest – by at least eight years - of 13 children: eight boys and five girls. My mother, Margaret, always managed to give birth to her children by herself – with the aid of a midwife, of course. As usual, the doctor summoned to help at my birth arrived too late.

Our farm, which my father, William, rented from his niece, was a mixed farm, with cattle, sheep, pigs, geese, turkeys, chickens, horses and so on – even, of course, rats. It comprised 210 acres.

● *Edgar's mother, Margaret, making butter.*

The farm is still in my family today. It is run by my nephew, Vernon Griffiths, the son of my sister Hannah.

Our farmhouse – a large building, constructed in 1870 - had two interconnected 'sections'. One of the sections contained the 'posh' rooms, while the rest of the house contained the more functional rooms of a working farmhouse.

My brothers helped my father to work the farm. However, since my father believed passionately in the power and value of education, several of my brothers left Cwrt Farm in order to pursue their studies.

My eldest brother, Simon, became an auctioneer in Cardigan.

My brother, Vernon (Vernie), also became an auctioneer – but in Newcastle Emlyn. His son is Professor Dr Leonard Evans MSc PhD DSc, currently Registrar of the University of Buckingham.

My third brother, Evan, died at home in 1917, aged 28, from a disease of the blood. He was a very nice man who was very keen on, and developed great skills in working with, horses. He won a great many prizes for his Shire horses. He also found time for me. In particular, I remember him taking me to collect hazelnuts – and I could not have been more than five years old.

Like Vernie, my brother John – known as Jack – was in the army during the Great War. Jack was one of twins. His twin brother, Samuel, only lived a few months.

In the War, Vernie served in Palestine, while Jack served in France. When Evan died, Vernon came home from Palestine and brought with him a wreath, which was made of glass and mother of pearl, to put on Evan's grave.

After the War, Jack wanted to own his own farm, so he became a smallholder in Llanfyllyn.

My brother, David (or Dai), stayed on the farm and became my father's 'right hand man'. He was to have quite a part to play in laying the foundations for my operatic career.

William (Will) was keen on chickens and went to Harper Adams College, a college which specialised in studying livestock. Eventually, he worked for the Ministry of Agriculture as the 'small livestock officer' for Wales, and lived in Aberystwyth. He and his wife had two daughters, Mary and Lynne.

My eldest sister, Elizabeth, married and had three children: Megan, Cyril and Howard. Hannah also married and had two children: Eddie, who runs a large farm near Whitland, in Cardiganshire, and Vernon, who now owns Cwrt Farm.

My sister, Sarah, went into service, in London, working for Lord Wimbourne. She married one of Lord Wimbourne's footmen – who was called George.

Another sister, Maggie, went to college in Aberystwyth and studied domestic science. She married Goronwy 'Gonny' Davies, the son of a cabinet maker in Llanybydder. Gonny's father had his own furniture shop in Llanybydder. Maggie and Gonny had two children: Irene, who married, had a daughter, Penny, and died of cancer while still relatively young, and Gerald, who went on to found a highly popular English language newspaper in Spain.

Gonny ran the electricity business in Llanybydder. The enormous generator included a huge wheel which was driven by a gas fired boiler. Eventually Gonny's generating business was taken over by the National Grid – and he concentrated on running the local Post Office.

My sister, Rachel, stayed on the farm for quite a while. However, a couple of years after my father had died – in April 1927, at the age of 69 - Hannah was getting married and it had been agreed that she and her husband would take over running the farm.

So Dai decided to leave and, around 1930, he bought a milk round in Clapham, south London. Rachel went to London to keep house for him.

My mother stayed on at the farm – and lived there until she died, at the age of 82, in 1947.

When I was old enough, I went to the local school in Pentre Cwrt Newydd (New Court village). The lessons were delivered through the medium of English and Welsh – but most lessons were conducted in English. The headmaster of the school was a Mr Davies. He was renowned as a poet and had won many 'chairs' at National Eisteddfodau.

While I was at that school – I would have been eight years old – my uncle, who was married to my mother's sister, Sarah, brought a wireless to the farm one day.

He was a superintendent in the Post Office and so broadcast

● *Scenes of Cwrt Newydd before the First World War.*

technology was part of his job. The wireless that he brought to show us was little better than a 'cat's whisker' but it had two dials and there was great excitement as we erected the aerial. This aerial had to be strung from one tree to another tree and, finally, brought into the house and attached to the wireless.

He fiddled around with the dials for a while and found a station. We heard our first broadcast. It was 1921 and the scene was set to fire me with the ambition to become an opera singer.

One evening, we invited our neighbours to come to Cwrt Farm to hear the radio – and they came along. However, that night – try as he might – my uncle could not find a station. So all we heard was a lot of 'static'. As our neighbours were leaving, my father asked one of the men what he had thought of the wireless. He said – in Welsh: "It's like a bumble bee inside a tin can!"

The next night, we found a station. It was a broadcast of Enrico Caruso singing at Covent Garden. This was the first time I heard Caruso and I was immediately captivated.

I thought that the word 'Garden' meant flowers and palm trees and, because the idea struck me that to sing among the flowers and palm trees must be a wonderful thing, I turned to my aunt and said: "Dyna le r'wyf am fod." ("That's where I want to be.")

I said to my father what a wonderful singer I thought Caruso was and, although I had thought of being a singer before I heard that broadcast, hearing Caruso's voice settled my mind on the career I wanted in life.

Of course, my father thought that my idea of being a singer was completely unrealistic – and he told me to forget about it!

● *On holiday in Newquay, Cardiganshire: Edgar (aged four) with his parents and brother Will.*

Chapter five

School, singing – and snogging on the organ stool

Years went by but, as I worked on the farm – in the seclusion of the barns - I would imitate in my own way the declamatory style of the preachers that I heard, Sunday by Sunday, in the local Unitarian chapel. And I would try to use that style in singing too.

By the time I was nine years old, I was top of my class at school in Pentre Cwrt Newydd. Then I went into the 'senior' class – which was taught by Mr Davies. Unfortunately for my fellow pupils and me, Mr Davies was more concerned with writing his prize-winning poetry. So he was more interested in keeping us children quiet in class while he got on with writing. Consequently neither I nor anyone else in the class made much progress in their last year at the school.

So I was pleased to leave the village school and go to Llandysul County School. I made some progress there – but not as much as I should have, perhaps because I had not had much teaching during my last year at the school in Cwrt Newydd. Consequently, I was sent to Newquay School, a private boarding school where my parents had to pay for everything, including my food and lodgings. The school itself was built like a big shed and the building rested on piles of bricks. Mr Jones – a small man - ran the school. His daughter, Dora, also taught in the school.

It was here that I began to get involved in singing – and made more progress in terms of music than in the more academic subjects.

In class I sat at the back of the room, next to a boy named Sam Rees.

One day, in class, Sam was engrossed in writing a letter. Dora Jones walked up to him and asked: "What are you doing, Sam?"

"I'm writing a letter to 'Ford's' of Dagenham," Sam said.

"Why?"

"To try to get a job there."

"Well, I'll help you then," she said – and she did. Not only did she help Sam to compose a letter which got him a job, it also ensured him a successful career – since he ended up being a director of Ford's.

● *Newquay School, 1929. Edgar is 11th from the left in the third row; Sam Rees is third from the left in the third row. Mr Jones, the headmaster (with moustache) is seated, centre; his daughter Dora is seated next to him on his left.*

Towards the end of my time at Newquay School – when I was 17 – I went to London to sit a 'bank exam' for the National & Provincial Bank. It was my first visit to London and, so, my brother Will came with me.

My brother Simon, the auctioneer, had a lot of dealings with the National & Provincial Bank in Cardiganshire and had arranged for me to be invited to sit the exam. As it turned out, I did badly in the exam – I was, perhaps, put off by the exuberant and rowdy antics of the other boys who were also there to sit the exam. After a while, I was called in to an office. A banker was looking at me sternly.

"What makes you think you could be a banker?" he barked.

"I don't really want to be a banker. I want to be a singer," I said.

"Well go back to Wales and be a singer. We don't want your sort in the bank!" I was told.

While I was at Newquay School, I started to take singing seriously. I found an accompanist. She was called Isabelle and lived a few doors away from where I was lodging with a Mrs Harding. Isabelle taught me songs by playing the piano and singing the song. Since I couldn't read music, I copied what she sang. In that way, she taught me some songs which I sang – as a baritone – in front of a large crowd of people during the school's end-of-year concert, held in a hall in Newquay.

My earlier singing debut – at a local eisteddfod as a 'boy soprano' – had been a disaster because I could not sing like a boy soprano. Trying to sound like a cross between Caruso and the Unitarian preachers, my vocal delivery was more like a man than a boy and my range was more baritonal than soprano. No wonder I had not done well. Things were different when I sang in the concert at Newquay.

I only sang in two eisteddfodau – one when I was aged 11 and the other when I was 20. My first attempt – in 1923, in the Sunday School building attached to the Unitarian Church in Capel y Bryn, Cwrt Newydd – had been a bit of a disappointment.

I was much more successful nine years later.

On this latter occasion, I remember walking the two miles or so from our farm to the chapel – Capel y Groes. It was a cold night and my mother had said to me, as I set out: "Keep your scarf around your neck. You know what to do when you sing. Have a piece of ginger to chew on the way - to keep the cold away before you go on to sing."

All the singers had to enter the 'solo twps' (fool's solo) category and, if they passed this test, they could go on to enter the other categories.

This time, I not only won the 'solo twps' class, but also the 'baritone solo' and 'champion solo' categories. I sang from the pulpit in the chapel, with the pianist - and piano - just below me. The place was packed with people. The adjudicator came from Fforest Fach and, coming from the 'valleys' rather than from the West Wales farming community, he knew a bit about singing. He must have been impressed with my vocal ability, especially since I had won three prizes at the one eisteddfod because he said, of me: "This boy has a wonderful voice and knows how to put it over. I advise him to go to London and have his voice trained."

I took this man's advice seriously.

After I finished my studies at Newquay School, I was articled in the County Architects' Office in Llandysul. I travelled to and from the office by bus, from my home in Cwrt Farm. My job involved going to visit various sites with the County Architect, named Rhys Jones FRIBA. He would take measurements and I would write them down for him. I did this for two years – and no wages at all!

While I was at Newquay School, I started to sing with a choir – comprising elderly men and me – at Towyn Chapel, in Newquay. The others in the choir were rather 'shy' of singing out, so they encouraged me to sing out because they could then join in with more confidence. This choir sang mainly hymns and, because the tenor part was not too high, I started to sing tenor. It was my introduction to singing as a tenor – although when I sang solos, I still sang as a baritone.

In those days, I also became friendly with a girl who was competing in an eisteddfod at Temple Bar chapel, near Newquay. I wasn't competing but I went with her, to wish her well. It was an eye-opener to me – to see what went on at a 'real' eisteddfod.

Later, I got friendly with Ina Peters. She was a young lady who was not only a daughter of the locally famous Captain Peters, of the P&O Line, but also the organist at a Calvinistic Methodist (Presbyterian) chapel. She enlisted my help in operating the organ bellows while she practised the organ. I was happy to do this because she was a very attractive young lady and I was involved - in however lowly a way – with music.

One afternoon, Ina was practising the organ – with my help. I was pumping away, out of sight of the organ console, when suddenly the organ fell silent. I kept pumping for a while, wondering why the organ wasn't making a sound. Eventually, I came out from behind the organ to find that a young man had arrived and he and Ina were kissing on the organ stool. When Ina noticed me, she quickly sent the young man on his way and got back to practising the organ.

I must have been a late developer. I was 17 or 18 years old and, until that moment, thoughts of sex had never really entered my head!

Eventually, I had to leave Newquay and go back to Cwrt Newydd.

There was no permanent job for me at the County Architects' Office; I had no money, and I was devoting all my energies to singing. Then things began to dawn on me: where and how was I going to earn my living?

At the end of my schooldays in Newquay, I decided to take refuge on the farm. After all, there was always plenty of food there! So I went back – and did my stint as a farm worker, with my brother, Dai.

Chapter six

Counting chickens

One day – about 1930 – I was working, with my brother Dai, in a field on our farm. The field was known as 'Cae (field) [of] Peace' – or, maybe 'Cae Peas'. I was never sure since I only ever heard the name pronounced. I never saw it written down!

Some time before, we had cut the corn and put the corn into stacks in the field. Then there was a terrible storm. It had not only soaked the corn but destroyed the stacks we had made. So Dai and I had gone to the field to re-stack the corn. I remember that there were also a lot of thistles in the field – and, since we were working without gloves, we had to use needles later to take the thistle thorns out of our hands.

As I was working in this field, I heard a voice – as plain as anything. It said: "What are you doing? Why don't you take up singing?"

I ran across to Dai – who was at the other end of the field – and asked him if he had heard a voice. Naturally, he said he hadn't.

At the time, that incident meant a lot to me – and it made me determined to embark on a career as a singer.

Of course, I couldn't leave the farm immediately. One day, my brother Will who, by that time, was the small livestock officer for Wales said to me: "Why don't you start a poultry farm?"

I replied: "Because I don't know anything about how to be a poultry farmer. I want to be a singer."

"Well," said Will, "you'll go to London and you'll only be able to sing in the street, cap in hand!"

The upshot was that Will helped me to establish a poultry farm – in one of the fields adjoining the farmhouse. I had a chicken house built in the field – and I had an incubator for the chicks to hatch.

Then my sister, Hannah, married David 'Dai' Griffiths and he took over the farm. Dai Griffiths allowed me to continue with the poultry farm. I was living in the farmhouse with my mother at this time – and it was about this time, when I was 17 or 18, that I had the first of several bouts of stones in the kidney.

The chicks - including a cockerel - which I bought to start my poultry farm came from Yorkshire. They came by rail to Llanybydder and I went to collect them.

Subsequently, I grew the farm by hatching 36 chicks from my incubator on a regular basis.

I ran the chicken farm for some four years – by which time, Hannah and Dai (Griffiths) had started a family - and Vernon Griffiths, who now runs Cwrt Farm, had been born.

One day, when Vernon was a little boy, he was taken ill with a severe chest problem. There was no telephone that we could use and so I had to ride a pony that we had on the farm all the way to Llanybydder to get the doctor to come to see him. The journey – there and back – was six miles.

By then, my brother Dai had gone into the milk business in London, principally because he could not have the same status on the farm that he had enjoyed when he ran the farm on behalf of my father.

Dai's living in London was an encouragement to me – because I could go to stay with him and try my hand at singing for a living. So, in 1934, I sold up my poultry farm – my brother Simon came back to conduct the auction – and set off for London. I took with me a small legacy, which I had received from my father, and the proceeds of the sale of my poultry farm. I had some money in my pocket but I had no promise of work of any kind from anyone.

Chapter seven

Impromptu impressions

When I came up to London in 1934, I had had to leave my girlfriend, Ina, behind in Cwrt Newydd. Ina worked in the local Post Office and, for some time, had been a regular visitor to my poultry farm.

Since we had developed a close relationship, it wasn't long before Ina made the trip to London to see me. She wanted me to start my own milk business – since having your own milk business in London was thought, by those in Cwrt Newydd and its environs, to be the way to get rich.

I told her that I had come to London to be a singer and I wasn't going to give up that ambition – and this was before I had auditioned for the Sadler's Wells Opera.

In the end, we couldn't agree and we parted - amicably. Ina didn't go back to Cardiganshire, though. After our relationship ended, Ina met, and later married, a London builder and decorator.

Some years later, when I was a member of the Royal Opera, I met the soprano, Victoria Sladen. Victoria said to me: "I know of an old flame of yours, called Ina.

"She had a terrible accident," she continued. "She was walking down a street in London, by some building works, and a piece of scaffolding fell down on top of her. She was taken to hospital but there was nothing anyone could do – and she died there. Her last words were, 'Tell Edgar I still love him.'"

Ina would have been in her early 40s when she died.

I only knew this because Ina's husband had gone to do some work for Victoria. Knowing that she was an opera singer, he asked her if she knew Edgar Evans. When she said that she did, he told her the story and asked her to let me know.

On arriving in London in 1934, I thought that my first task was to find a singing teacher.

However, that had to wait because, first, England played Wales in a rugby international at Twickenham. My brother and I were never very 'sporty' but we all decided to go to the match (which ended in a 3 - 3 draw, with England scoring a penalty goal to Wales' try).

We didn't have tickets – so we, and a lot of other people, didn't get in to the ground. We decided to go back home – to Landor Road, Clapham – but promised to meet up with some of our new friends, who had also failed to get into the ground, later that evening at Ward's Irish House in Piccadilly.

Since no one – especially Wales – had lost, we all had a really good time. The party was in full swing when a group of us started to sing. The man standing next to me said: "You've got a good voice there!"

The place was crowded, so I was hauled up on to a table to sing to the whole place. Unaccompanied, I sang – completely inappropriately but it was the only song I could remember at the time – 'Loch Lomond'.

After I had finished singing, the man was still impressed. He turned out to be young doctor – and he said to me: Come with me, boy."

In the end, six of us – including the doctor – went in a taxi to a club in Conduit Street, called 'The Odd Spot'. It was not a big club but, judging by the clientele there, it seemed to be 'exclusive'. Again, I was encouraged to sing. I sang – in a baritone key – the song, 'Until'.

The doctor then introduced me to the manager of Rolls Royce who said: "I know someone called Arthur Fagg, who is the conductor of the London Choral Society. I'll give you his telephone number. I'm sure he'll be able to help you."

On the way home, one of our group of six – which had not included my brother, Dai – had to get to an underground station in order to get a train home. When the taxi stopped outside the station, we saw a man who was so drunk that he couldn't move. I called a taxi and put the man in it and, having found out from the drunk where he wanted to go, told the taxi driver where to take him.

Some three years later, I met Nan Walters – my wife to be – for the first time. It was on the steps of King's Cross (Welsh Congregational) Chapel after a service – at which the Rev Elfed Lewis had preached. Nan had been working as a nanny and had just returned from Spain, where she had been looking after the child of the artist, Mark Gertler.

Nan was talking to a blonde girl on the steps and I said to my brother, Dai: "She looks lovely."

I beckoned to them and they both walked towards us. I asked Nan if she'd like to come with us. She agreed and we went to a Lyons Corner House, where Dai and I had mashed potatoes and sausages – at a cost of 2/6d (12.5p). Nan said she didn't want anything to eat but she was happy to chat to me while Dai and I ate.

Later, when we were making preparations for our wedding, Nan said to me: "I've got a brother called Edgar, like you."

I replied: "Years ago, I met a chap called Edgar after I'd been to the Irish House in Piccadilly. He was so drunk I put him in a taxi and got the driver to take him home."

"I don't think it would have been my brother," said Nan – but she was wrong. It was.

Edgar Walters – Nan's brother – was a major in the Army. He had just returned from a tour of duty in India when I met him that night I sang at the Irish House and The Odd Spot.

One of the six of us who went on to The Odd Spot that night was Lawton Davies, who was private secretary to Lloyd George. He was the only one of the group with whom I kept in touch – and I did so for years. Oddly enough, he also kept in touch with Nan's brother Edgar – although he knew of him in a different context to knowing him to be my wife's brother. The world is full of odd coincidences.

As soon as I could, I telephoned Arthur Fagg. He told me: "I'm not a singing teacher but I can recommend Dawson Freer as a good teacher. He's currently teaching at the Royal College of Music."

And he gave me Dawson Freer's telephone number.

Chapter eight

Further and Freer

So I phoned Dawson Freer, who asked me to come to see him, privately, at the Wigmore Studios. He rented a room there twice a week.

I arrived at the studios and went in to see Mr Freer. He asked me what I was going to sing. I had learnt the song 'Until' - mainly by listening to a recording of it by Frank Titterton, a tenor who sang in the style of Walter Widdup. Incidentally, some years later - when I was in the chorus at Sadler's Wells and living with my wife, Nan, in the top flat at 21 Adelaide Road in Hampstead, with Edith Coates and Harry Lloyd living in the rest of the house - we heard Frank Titterton sing the part of Calaf in Turandot, in a performance broadcast on radio.

Having sung 'Until', Dawson Freer delivered his verdict.

"Your voice is too loud. And you're not a baritone. You're a tenor."

When I went to Dawson Freer I had a large, natural voice. After six months with him, I lost my voice. The sound I was making wasn't 'me' at all! Dawson Freer blamed the London traffic and the smog but it was only an excuse.

He tried to get me to sing by 'placing' my voice above the bridge of my nose – in a place that Peter Pears called 'the imposto'. Peter Pears sang that way – he didn't know any other way to sing. But there is another way – a way which I discovered almost too late in my career.

Another of Freer's singing pupils was the soprano, Joan Cross.

Although the style and technique of singing that he taught was not very good, Dawson Freer was a good teacher because he kept you interested in singing artistically 'good' music.

The accompanist for my audition with Dawson Freer was Cecil Belcher and, after I had become a member of the Sadler's Wells chorus, I asked Cecil if he could help me to learn some more songs. So he used to come to Adelaide Road, where I was living – and where I had a piano. He played the piano for me and taught me some songs. In return, I paid him a guinea for a couple of hours work.

I then took these songs along to Dawson Freer, so that he could work on my voice. I had to have someone like Cecil to work with me 'in the background' because I couldn't read music – so I had to know all the notes of a song before I went to 'learn it' with Dawson Freer.

I kept this 'musical dyslexia' secret all my working life but, during my career, I met many other professional singers – both from the UK and from the Continent - who were as musically dyslexic as I was.

The first song that Dawson Freer asked me to work on for him was 'Hark, the echoing air a triumph sings' – a song from Purcell's 'The Faerie Queene'. It was quite a different song from the songs I had been used to singing!

Later, he gave me a series of songs to learn but I didn't really want to learn them. I wanted to sing operatic arias – but Dawson Freer would not allow me to sing them because, he said, he didn't want me to over-work my voice.

The voice that Dawson Freer had manufactured for me enabled me to get a contract at Sadler's Wells, kept me going through the concerts I sang during the War and helped me to get into the company at the Royal Opera House. My 'natural' voice only returned after David Webster had sent me to study – briefly – under the Italian maestro, Ricci, in Rome in 1950. Ricci helped me to

● *Luigi Ricci and his son.*

rediscover an 'open' sound in my voice that had been suppressed by the 'covered' sound, produced from the sinuses, which Dawson Freer had championed.

Nonetheless, in those early days, Dawson Freer used to tell me, repeatedly: "Believe me, Evans, this is how the Italians sing."

How wrong he was. However, he was a very intelligent man who had had a career as a baritone before going to teach at the Royal College of Music. He was certainly revered in the music world in the years immediately preceding the War.

Finally, Dawson Freer allowed me to learn 'Spirito gentil', from Donizetti's La Favorita. I was delighted at being allowed to sing an operatic aria. Unfortunately – largely owing to the vocal technique that Dawson Freer was giving me – I could never sing the top note and, consequently, could never finish the aria.

However, Dawson Freer got me to sing competently in this style – although it was a great physical effort for me to do so. Nonetheless, I found it very difficult to sing above a top 'A' – and my attempts to do so did not always meet with success!

My persistence with Dawson Freer and his method of singing paid off, though. I had first gone to see him in 1936. After I had been his pupil for some 18 months, Dawson Freer arranged an audition for me – for the chorus at Sadler's Well Opera.

Chapter nine

Milk with music

For that year or so – 1936/37 – I had to have a job in order to live. However, I had no qualifications – only a voice which was none too good. So I got a job as a milkman with the Royal Arsenal Co-Operative Society.

The job came about because my brother, Dai, had a milk business in south London. My brother Dai had a better voice – he was a baritone - than I had but he didn't have the determination to 'make it' to the top of the singing profession.

One day, Dai was talking about me to a roundsman from a rival company who said: "Then tell Edgar to go to the Royal Arsenal Co-Op's depot in Camberwell Green and see Mr Birkett, the depot manager. Tell Edgar to give Birkett £5 and he'll give him a job."

So I borrowed £5, went to see Mr Birkett – and got the job.

Mr Birkett made quite a good business out of giving people jobs at the dairy and pocketing their five pounds. Eventually, he was caught out – while I was working for the dairy.

Four roundsmen, including me, were summoned to the company's headquarters where each of us, in turn, had to be interviewed by a panel of senior managers. I was the last of the four of us to go in to see these managers and, before I went, I saw the third man to be interviewed – who was called Reeves. So I asked him: "What did you say?"

"I said I had given Birkett money."

So I went in to see the senior managers. They asked me if I had given Mr Birkett any money to get my job with the dairy.

"None whatsoever," I lied.

It was the biggest lie I ever told – but I was desperate to keep my job. The other three who had been interviewed – and had all agreed that they had given Mr Birkett some money in order to get their jobs – were sacked. Mr Birkett also left the Co-Op's employ. I was kept on and continued to work as an 'auxiliary milkman'.

This meant that I did the rounds of any 'real' milkman who was ill. Of course, that meant that I never knew where I would be delivering milk. So not only was I unsure of the geography of the area but I also didn't know which houses wanted milk from me. The dairy foreman used to come out with me on the first day of each new round, to make sure that I delivered the right amount of milk to all the right places. Of course, having completed the round once, I knew that route subsequently.

Some of the rounds were enormous.

Each milkman had a three-wheeled cart, loaded with crates of milk, along with butter and eggs. He pushed this – up hill and down dale – along his round. Fully loaded, the cart weighed half a ton. It was certainly very heavy to push!

I suppose you could say that I've always worked with royalty. I started working for the Royal Arsenal Co-Op, then the Royal Opera and finally the Royal College of Music!

At the end of my first week as a milkman, I learnt that you had to balance the books on a Saturday. If the customers hadn't paid you for their milk, butter or eggs, then you had to make up the difference out of your own pocket. My rounds were often in the East End of London – and the people there were past masters at avoiding having to pay me!

However, I learnt fast and soon discovered who were the good – and the bad – payers. I made sure that the good payers paid for the bad payers. What else could I do in order to get the books to balance?

Some of the customers on my rounds used dreadful language – saying 'f***ing' this and that all the time. It was quite a shock to a country boy from Cardiganshire.

I was a milkman for 14 months – until I landed the job in the chorus at Sadler's Wells Opera. All this time I was living with my brother, Dai – who, some while later, came to a tragic end: he was killed by a lorry in south London.

Apparently, the driver of the lorry lost control of his vehicle and drove into Dai. A passer by – who witnessed the accident – ran until he found a policeman and told him that there had been an accident back down the road. The policeman went to the scene of the accident, only to discover that it was his father – Dai – who had been fatally injured. So, through a strange coincidence, my nephew – David - was able to say 'goodbye' to his father before Dai died. Incidentally, the lorry driver was never found.

I owe a great debt to my brother, Dai. He was kind and generous to everybody but especially to me – including letting me live with him in London for free. He had a heart of gold and everybody loved him.

By 1937, he had moved to new premises on the Stockwell Road. Once I had become a member of the Sadler's Wells Opera, I became something of a local celebrity there – chiefly because everyone knew about the founder of the company: Lilian Baylis.

When I was an auxiliary milkman, I used to have a bicycle – which had very thin wheels (and no brakes except for the pedals). So, on a wet day, the front tyre would easily slip off the road and into the gap in the middle of the tramline track, which took some of the electricity which powered the trams (the circuit was completed by the tram being connected to the overhead cable). When the tyre became caught in this way, the bike would be lodged in this track up to the hub of the front wheel and it was difficult to get the bike out again! There was also the danger that a tram would come along and, at the very least, your bike would be trapped and then mangled by the tram.

I had to be at work for 5am at the latest. So I had to get up at 4am and – without having breakfast – cycle from Landor Road, Clapham (or, later, Stockwell Road) to the dairy. My first meal of the day was when I pulled up at a pavement café during my round. I would have a mug of strong tea – which included soda in order to 'get more out of the tea leaves' – and sugar, followed by two rounds of toast and dripping.

There was a big building on the Stockwell Road to which my

brother, Dai, delivered milk. As a result, he became friendly with the manager at this building – whose name was Ted Basted. He may have had the surname 'Basted' but he was one of the kindest men I ever met.

I got to know Ted quite well and, one day, he introduced me to the mother of Geraldo, the famous dance band leader. Geraldo's mother lived in the Stockwell Road area too. At this time, she wanted to sell an old piano, a carpet and a vacuum cleaner. I needed a piano, so I bought the lot – for £12.

Although both the piano and vacuum cleaner have long gone, the carpet is still in use (in 2005 – some 70 years later). It is in the house in the Lake District used in the summertime by my dear son, Huw, and his family – until Huw's death from cancer, (on 24th June 1999). Their son – my grandson – Edward now lives there, since it is convenient to where he now works.

Once, I asked Ted: "Why not change your name from 'Basted'?"

Ted replied: "I've tried to change it, but I really can't!"

So Ted Basted he remained.

He was kind enough to give me his old radiogram when he was getting a new one. That radiogram was invaluable because I used it to learn new songs – principally from the recordings and broadcasts of singers including many tenors, such as Frank Titterton and Gigli – who became one of my all-time favourite tenors.

By now, I had a room of my own – and I could afford to buy my own bed. It was brand new and cost £2/10/- (£2.50 in today's money). And when I went home to Wales to see my mother, she gave me some blankets and bed linen for the bed.

I gave my audition for Sadler's Wells Opera in the spring of 1937. I sang 'Sigh no more, ladies' and 'Hark, the echoing air a triumph sings'. On the audition panel was Lilian Baylis and the company's musical director, Lawrance Collingwood, Geoffrey Corbett, the chorus master, and Lilian Baylis' secretary. I came to have a lot of

● *Lawrance Collingwood.*

33

time for Lawrance Collingwood, the main conductor at Sadler's Wells. He was a very strict but also a very fair man – and a thorough professional.

At the end of the audition, they said: "Thanks. We'll let you know."

It didn't sound too promising but, soon afterwards, I received a letter from Lilian Baylis offering me the job and telling me to contact the company's librarian to get some music to learn.

I joined the company in September and was soon on stage – singing in the chorus in Mascagni's Cavalleria Rusticana.

It was a great feeling to be singing in opera. I was doing what I wanted to do. The only problem was that I didn't want to be in the chorus.

Anyway, I was very grateful to Lilian Baylis and her team. They had helped me to get away from having to push a barrow loaded with dairy products – which had been absolute hell.

The operas came and went. I became friendly with my colleagues. There was no 'snobbishness' among the singers in the company: both the chorus and the principals mixed well together. I discovered that my chorus colleague, Bruce Dargavel, shared my musical dyslexia. It was a discovery that made me less nervous and encouraged me to think that I could do well as an opera singer despite this disability.

There were eight men in the chorus of the Sadler's Wells Opera: two basses, two baritones (one of which was Bruce Dargavel), two second tenors and two first tenors. I was engaged as one of the second tenors.

Geoffrey Corbett, the chorus master and an assistant conductor with the company, taught us our parts in the operas.

From time to time, we were expected to fill in as extras for the Sadler's Wells Ballet too. The singers would play a group of villagers who, generally, decorated the stage as on-stage onlookers while the dancing was going on. In one ballet - Barabow, a French ballet, starring Margot Fonteyn - there was a requirement for a small chorus, in which I sang.

● *Geoffrey Corbett.*

Indeed, my first appearance on the stage at Covent Garden occurred when I was being an extra – holding some sort of prop which I dimly recall might have been a spear - in one of these ballets. The occasion was a special gala performance by the Sadler's Wells Ballet at Covent Garden, with the French President – Monsieur Le Brun - as guest of honour. I think that the ballet performed was Diaghilev's The Sleeping Princess. It was conducted by Sir Thomas Beecham and featured Margot Fonteyn, Harold Turner, Lesley Edwards and, probably, Frederick Ashton.

Chapter ten

War work

After my 'debut' in the Sadler's Wells' chorus in Cavalleria Rusticana, I became one of the priests in Aida – singing, for the first of many times in my career, alongside Bruce Dargavel (who was another member of our profession whom I admired).

While we were on stage, waiting to appear in Aida, Henry Robinson, the stage manager, spotted me.

"Who made you up?" he asked me.

"No one. I did it myself," I replied, proudly.

"Well, you look like George Robey!" he said. "Go and change your make up!"

He was probably right. I had no idea how to 'make up' to appear on the stage. Despite 'curtain up' being imminent, Bruce Dargavel went with me back to the dressing room and helped me take off the make up that I had applied; then he made me up properly.

It was Henry Robinson who, nearly ten years later, was to change my life by encouraging me to audition for the Royal Opera.

The main parts in the Sadler's Wells' Aida were taken by John (Jack) Wright (Radames), Molly de Gunst (Aida), Edith Coates (Amneris) and Redvers Llewellyn (Amonasro). Jack Wright stood six feet three inches (almost two metres) tall. He looked 'right' for the part of Radames. He had a good voice too – but there were 'restrictions' in it which prevented him achieving the 'open', Italianate sound required of a Verdi tenor.

I thoroughly enjoyed the 1937/38 season at Sadler's Wells and returned for the 1938/39 season – but then, when the War began in September 1939, the theatres began closing and the Sadler's Wells company was broken up. Many of them went north, where there was still a chance to do some singing in the theatres there. The alternatives were to join the armed services or other organisations such as the police or the Local Defence Volunteers/Home Guard.

At that time, I had a telephone call from a lady who asked if I would do some singing in hospitals. I agreed – and ended up doing a great many concerts, mainly in the London area.

I had also joined the Metropolitan Police and, because I kept being asked to sing in the hospital concerts, I kept asking for time off from my police duties. Eventually it became embarrassing – so I could only sing in the concerts on my days off from the police.

These concerts were a new experience for me. I hadn't done any concerts at all while I was at Sadler's Wells because I'd been fully employed at that theatre and hadn't had the time to sing in concerts.

I was paid £3 a week in the police – and took home £2/19/11d, because one penny went towards the state pension. That was the same amount as I had been taking home as a chorister at Sadler's Wells.

My fiancée, Nan, and I were married on 19th August 1939. We began our married life living in 'one room and a kitchen' at 96 Adelaide Road, Hampstead. It was a big house and almost everyone else living there – apart from the owner, who was English - were Jews from Czechoslovakia who had escaped from Nazi persecution.

I became friends with many of these people – but the 'regulars' among my colleagues in the police force hated them.

Very soon after the War began, the police took these Jews to internment camps. The Jews weren't allowed to own cars – or even bicycles. They had to give them up. One of the Jews owned a new, large Armstrong Siddeley car and, when the police came to take the Jew to internment, he accepted an offer to sell it – for £500 – to one of the policemen.

For the first few months of the War, I was based at Rochester Row

Police Station, off Vauxhall Bridge Road. Later, I transferred to Hampstead – principally because Nan and I were living in Hampstead. Nan was working as a nanny – looking after the children of the eminent Harley Street heart specialist, Dr Shirley Smith.

One day, I sang some popular ballads at a police concert. After the concert, a police superintendent from 'S' Division, based at Golders Green, said to me: "Doing a lot of singing is not conducive to being on the beat. How would you like to become an assistant in the Aliens' Office?"

Realising that this job – based on the first floor of Hampstead Police Station - would give plenty of time to sing in concerts, I agreed.

Working in the Aliens' Office, brought me into contact with a great many 'human interest' stories – and not many of them ended pleasantly. On one occasion, a young Jewish lady accompanied her much older husband to the office. Obviously apprehensive, the man was extremely nervous to the point of almost uncontrollable shaking.

The official decided that the old man had to go to an internment camp but his wife pleaded for him to stay at home, in order for him to receive the care that he needed. So the official – a detective – began to bargain with her.

"If I let him stay, will you let me come to see you?" he asked, euphemistically.

After some time – and some persistence on the part of the detective – the lady refused the detective's advances and her husband went to the internment camp.

I found that I had plenty of time to sing in concerts. I did an audition for ENSA – the invitation to audition for ENSA arose from my hospital concert work. Then the Arts Council – then known as CEMA – heard about me and asked if I would do something for them. The head of CEMA – who invited me to work for them – was a Miss Tatham. She was eventually superseded by Steuart – later Sir Steuart – Wilson (who, later, became deputy general administrator at Covent Garden, under David Webster).

Also, at the very end of the War in May 1946, Geoffrey Corbett who had been the chorus master at the Sadler's Wells Opera, asked Bruce Dargavel and me to sing in two operas which were to be performed at the Kings Cross Town Hall. One of the operas was called The

Ephesian Matron or The Widow's Tears and was written by Charles Dibdin. I sang the role of a Roman Centurion. We performed both The Ephesian Matron and The Partisans (in the same way as Cav and Pag are traditionally staged together) on four consecutive nights: 28th to 31st May. By then, I was singing a great many concerts with ENSA and CEMA, but this was my first chance to sing a solo part in opera.

The other opera was a contemporary English opera, written by Inglis Gundry and called The Partisans. It starred Esther Salaman. Our paths would cross again in the 1980s, when she and I, along with Constance Shacklock, agreed to be 'vice presidents' of Welwyn Opera, a group of largely amateur singers based in the Welwyn Garden City area of Hertfordshire. Esther conducted a masterclass for the group and she and I attended one or two of their performances.

● *With Esther Salaman in The Ephesian Matron.*

Esther Salaman was married to the vocal coach, Paul Hamburger. It was Paul Hamburger who taught me the difficult role of Boaz in Lennox Berkeley's opera, Ruth. The role of Boaz had been written for Peter Pears but, for some reason, he didn't sing it and I did it instead.

The part of Boaz was extremely difficult. In one place, I had to sing – for five pages of the score – unaccompanied and then the chorus had to follow that by beginning to sing on an E flat. It was absolutely essential that I kept in tune during my unaccompanied solo.

In rehearsal, I finished my solo and the conductor, who was Charles Mackerras, shouted: "You're flat!"

"No he isn't," said the accompanist, from the pit, and he played an E flat to prove it. Unfortunately, that was the last we saw of the accompanist.

I was delighted to be asked to sing one of the main parts in The Ephesian Matron (it was a lot easier than singing the part of Boaz turned out to be many years later!) but I wasn't sure if I could learn it. Thankfully, I now had a piano and so I could 'bash out the notes' to learn my part. In addition, Geoffrey Corbett coached me in the part too.

The performances were marvellous. There was a good audience for each performance and they gave us some enthusiastic applause. Several members of the audience congratulated me after the performances. One of these was Walter Glynne, a well known tenor before the War. In addition to saying 'well done', he said to me: "You've got a future."

It was a great encouragement – especially since I was still singing then in the 'Dawson Freer style'. It was style of singing that suited baritones and basses – and Dawson Freer had been a professional baritone before becoming a teacher. Indeed, many of the basses and baritones I came across during my career sang in this way. The exceptions to this were, mainly, the Italian singers – who knew better.

When I was teaching at the Royal College of Music, I had a pupil, called Jane Kamargue, who got a job singing in the chorus at Glyndebourne. From there, she went to work in Italy – and sang in the chorus at La Scala, Milan. From there, she wrote to me that: 'The Italians are teaching (singing) exactly what you've taught me.'

During the war, I went - for CEMA - with a pianist and violinist, to tour Somerset. One day, the pianist wanted to visit Wells Cathedral and postpone the concert we were scheduled to give. I objected – and got into trouble for it! I didn't want to go to visit a cathedral. I'd been engaged to give a concert – and I told the pianist so. When we got back to London, the pianist complained that I'd been making trouble and I was summoned before the CEMA board. Eventually, they decided to renew my contract with them for a further six months – on a sort of probationary period.

Over the six war years, I sang in all sorts of places – in hospitals and factories; for troops, the Red Cross and so on. I even visited Northern

● *On tour to Ireland, 1942 with Joyce Grenfell (seated far right) and Richard Addinsell (standing far right).*

Ireland - in November 1942.

I was there – in Northern Ireland - when my son, Huw, was born.

I had finished singing a song when my fellow CEMA performer, Joyce Grenfell, came on stage and announced to the audience that I had become a father. Immediately, I asked her – in front of the whole audience: "Is it a boy or a girl?"

"It's a boy," she said and there was warm applause from the audience.

On that tour, with Joyce Grenfell and myself, were Richard Addinsell, of Warsaw Concerto fame, who played the concerto to audiences every night; a very fine violinist called Alfred Cave, and a baritone called Harry Trevor whose professional name was 'Clifford Trevor'. In later years, Harry – or Clifford – changed his name again when he became a teacher of vocal technique. He became David Kerran and set up house, in Hampstead, with Stuart Nash, who was a fine accompanist. Indeed, Stuart Nash worked at the Royal College of Music while I was teaching there.

Harry/Clifford/David was the son of John Trevor, of Trevor & Sons, the auctioneers. A Jew by race but a Christian by religion, John Trevor raised over £1m for the War Effort – for which he was allegedly offered a knighthood but rejected the offer because he wanted a peerage instead. Needless to say, the peerage was never forthcoming.

When I met Harry first he was living in Inverness Terrace, off Lancaster Gate in London. There, he had a massive collection of records – all '78s' of course – of famous singers. He had catalogued each of these records in a large book and had had special, very large speakers made for his gramophone system. The speakers and the records completely filled a large room in his house.

He was very interested indeed in my voice and, soon after he started to teach vocal technique – shortly after I had started work at Covent Garden – he said that he thought that I could 'do better' with my voice.

"Come along," he said to me, "and I'll improve your singing."

So I went along to see him and sounded a few notes. Harry went into a deep reverie. He thought and thought – but he didn't make any suggestions about my vocal technique.

After the fifth of these 'lessons', Harry asked me for a fee. I replied: "Harry, you haven't taught me anything. You've spent some time with me but you haven't helped me produce a better sound."

So we parted – but we remained friends until I had started teaching at the Royal College of Music.

When I was at the Royal College of Music, I helped one of my students – called David – to get a one year, all tuition fees paid, scholarship to study singing. Instead of continuing to study with me, David – who later died of AIDS - went to study with Harry.

I wasn't at all worried about that. David was free to choose a tutor. However, the next year Harry asked me to get David another scholarship – and a further year's tuition fees. Of course, that was not within my gift – but it broke our friendship.

I got my discharge from the Metropolitan Police after 18 months service – around June 1942 (see page 154). In the end, I had asked to leave in order to go singing. However, very soon after that, I received my call-up papers and I reported to Edgware for my medical examination to join the armed forces.

At the medical examination – for which I was wearing hardly any clothes - I told the doctor that I wanted to join the RAF to be a rear gunner in a bomber. He completed my medical examination and then said: "Get down on your knees."

I did so, kneeling down in front of the doctor's desk – so that he could only see the upper half of my body.

Then he said: "Now jump up."

"I can't," I said.

"What are you taking about?" asked the doctor, surprised.

"I can't – and neither could you," I said – because I had got down on my knees with my feet pointing behind me, not 'curled up' with my toes pointing towards my knees.

The doctor didn't look at me – he was sitting behind his desk – or investigate this any further. Instead he sent me to a Harley Street doctor. The Harley Street doctor examined me thoroughly and then asked me to sit in the waiting room while he wrote a letter for me to take back to the first doctor.

The doctor's secretary gave me the envelope containing the letter. The gum on the envelope had not dried so, of course, as soon as I was back out on the street, I opened the letter easily. It said: 'Do not take this man for any of the armed forces. He is too highly strung and temperamental.'

I re-sealed the letter and returned to Edgware, where I handed the letter to the chief medical officer there. After reading the letter, he said: "Well, the best thing you could do is sing for the troops."

He classified me as 'C3' – and sing for the troops was what I did for the next four years or so.

At the medical examination, I had mentioned that I had had trouble with stones in the kidneys when I'd been 17 years old. These stones in the kidneys returned seven years later – and, indeed, at other times in my life subsequently. In all, I passed 21 kidney stones. These stones comprise calcium oxylate and have jagged edges. Passing them can be a very painful experience. The stones are formed because the parathyroid gland is overactive and too much calcium gets into the blood.

For a long time I was put on a low calcium diet. I could only drink a pint of milk a week and was forbidden chocolate and spinach! Nonetheless, despite all this attention to a strict diet, the stones still returned. Thankfully, I have not had a stone in the kidneys since 1980.

CEMA and ENSA kept me busy throughout the War. In all, I sang over 500 concerts for them. This had a number of benefits for me – not least that it strengthened my voice; got me used to a wide variety of audiences, and also got me used to performing even if I wasn't feeling too well.

At the end of the War, I joined the Anglo-Russian Merry Go Round under the auspices of ENSA as one of their two tenors (Patrick Howey was the other – and senior – tenor in the company).

I also performed in the first Opera for All performances, with CEMA. The other performers included Nina Barbone, the baritone Fabian Smith and a bass, named Henderson. We toured throughout the West Country – and opened the new Arts Theatre in Bridgewater, Somerset.

It was from there that I joined the opera company at Covent Garden.

● *Opera for All in Bridgewater, with Edgar as Basilio in The Marriage of Figaro.*

Chapter eleven

Chance and a cigarette packet

In 1945, I was understudying the parts of Alfred and Eisenstein in Gay Rosalinda at the Palace Theatre, in London. Bernard Delfont was the director and Richard Tauber was conducting. David Davies was playing the part of Eisenstein and James 'Jimmy' Etherington was Alfred and, although Jimmy almost wasn't well enough to do one performance, I never managed to get on the stage!

At the end of the show's run, Bernard Delfont asked me to do a summer show for him at Ryde, in the Isle of Wight.

I had nothing else to do – so I agreed.

The show was called The Gay Review and included such performers as Wilson, Kepple and Betty. I had the only 'decent' song in the show – called 'Gypsy Moon' – and it regularly brought the house down.

When Bernard Delfont and his colleagues, such as the show's director, Frank Adey, decided to change the contents of the show, I was sent to Fox's, in London, for a fitting for a new costume. I happened to pass the stage door of the Royal Opera House – and, indeed, I thought it was Fox's.

At the stage door, I saw Henry Robinson, whom I'd known at Sadler's Wells. We hadn't seen each other since 1939, when Henry had been the stage director at Sadler's Wells when I had been in the chorus there. He was now the stage director at Covent Garden and we greeted each other with open arms. We were delighted to see each other after all that time.

Henry asked me where I was working and what I was doing in London. I told him – and he pointed out where Fox's was. Then he said: "We're putting on a new opera company here. Why not have a go to get in to it? I tell you what, get that piece of paper on the floor, write your name and address on it and I'll pass it on for you."

So I wrote my application on the back of a cigarette packet and gave it to Henry.

A few days later, back in the Isle of Wight, I received a letter from Covent Garden inviting me to an audition. I went to the audition – and sang 'E lucevan l'estelle' from Tosca and the Flower Song from Carmen. All they said was: "Thank you very much."

● *Henry Robinson.*

A second letter came for me, inviting me to audition again. This time, I sang 'Che l'a mi creda' from Pucinni's Girl of the Golden West and 'O loveliness beyond compare' from Mozart's The Magic Flute. Again, they said: "Thank you very much."

Apparently, however, one of the secretaries at the Opera House – a Miss O'Donnell – had heard me singing and liked my voice. It was she who wrote to me to say that Karl Rankl wanted to hear me sing again.

I got a third letter. This one invited me to the 'final auditions for tenors'.

I was astonished when I got to the Opera House. There were at least 20 other tenors there to audition. Later, I was told that they had heard over 100 tenors and had made their choice from these.

I wasn't put off at all but I wondered who these people were. During wartime there hadn't been many professional singers – let alone tenors - about. Sadler's Wells Opera had spent the War being based in Burnley but professional operatic singers were few and far between in wartime Britain.

I sang 'E lucevan l'estelle' from Tosca and 'Che l'a mi creda' again – and went back to Ryde in the Isle of Wight. When I arrived, Frank

Adey told me that the show was going to finish in a fortnight's time. I heard nothing more from Covent Garden and so my wife, Nan, and I, along with our son, Huw, who was then about three years old, went back to see my mother at the farm at Cwrt Newydd, in Llanybydder, in Cardiganshire when I had been born and brought up.

One morning we were having breakfast when Ivor, the postman – he was the son of the local tailor – brought us some letters. One of them had the Royal Opera House crest on it. It was from David Webster, inviting me to join the Royal Opera as one of its three principal tenors.

Throughout the War, I had been working for ENSA and the Arts Council, doing various concerts and shows such as the Anglo-Russian Merry Go Round. Now, the Arts Council had offered me 12 weeks of work, touring the West Country doing scenes from operas including La Boheme and The Marriage of Figaro.

● Edgar in The Anglo-Russian Merry Go Round.

So I joined the Royal Opera in October 1946, once I had finished the Arts Council tour.

I was fortunate that the Royal Opera House took me on at the same salary as I had been getting with the Arts Council - £25 a week. And, as I continued at the Opera House, I'm delighted to say that my salary rose regularly and steadily.

The other two founding principal tenors of the company were Kenneth Neate, an Australian (or Canadian?) and Dennis Stephenson. Dennis and I were initially engaged to do the comprimario parts. These were always shared because it was a repertory company for British singers, with a few foreigners coming in now and again.

Kenneth Neate was not a good actor – which didn't please the Opera House – and he didn't think that the Opera House paid him enough money. So he didn't stay very long. Instead, he made a good career for himself on the Continent.

Dennis Stephenson proved to be not up to standard as an operatic tenor.

One of the established guest artists at Covent Garden was the tenor, Heddle Nash. Indeed, it was because Heddle Nash was unwell one evening in 1947 that I made my debut - on 25th March 1947 – as the Chevalier des Grieux in Manon Lescaut.

According to Gladys Davidson's 'Opera Biographies', published in 1955: 'He made his Covent Garden debut in the important role of the Chevalier des Grieux in Massanet's Manon, in which he created an excellent impression.'

However, strictly speaking, I had made my debut at Covent Garden in 1946, playing two parts – the God of the Birds and The Lover in Purcell's The Faerie Queene – but des Grieux was my first major operatic role there.

[Indeed, many years later, Sir Michael Hordern, who was one of Edgar's co-performers in The Faerie Queene, commented to me on what a thoroughly enjoyable production that had been.]

Chapter twelve

Dyslexia and Dancairo

I can't understand how I got on so well with all the many conductors with which I worked in my career – including Erich Kleiber, Karl Rankl, Sir Thomas Beecham, Sir John Barbirolli, Sir Malcolm Sargent, Sir Georg Solti, Otto Klemperer, Rudolf Kempe and Carlo Maria Giulini.

I was dyslexic musically. I couldn't read music without a piano to help me.

To sing for all these great musicians and never have any trouble with them! It was only because I had worked hard and learnt my part to perfection before I ever went to a rehearsal.

Only once was I ever asked to go on, unprepared. It happened during my first season at Covent Garden, in 1946. The singer who was singing the role of El Dancairo, one of the chief smugglers in Carmen, was indisposed. The performance was being conducted by Karl Rankl and I got a phone call from Patrick Terry, the then manager of the company, who said: "Edgar, will you go along to Holborn Town Hall where they are rehearsing Carmen, because Graham Clifford has been taken ill."

I said: "But Dancairo's a baritone. I'm a tenor."

Patrick replied: "But the role is sometimes done by a tenor."

"Well, I'm not going to do it," I said – knowing full well that I couldn't sing the part because I hadn't learnt it.

"Rankl says you have to do it," said Patrick.

A short while later, I received a phone call from the opera company's administrator, David Webster, who said: "Come and see me, now."

I went to see David Webster – and took the score of Carmen with me.

Again, we went through the conversation of 'why are you not going to sing this part?'

"You've taken me on as a tenor but it says in the score that Dancairo is a baritone," I said, showing him the score.

"You've only been here five or six weeks and already you're creating trouble within the company," David Webster said.

"I'm not creating anything of the sort!" I retorted.

Sure enough, I got away with it – so my lack of 'music reading ability' was never discovered. I would have been caught out for sure if I had ever had to do anything like that. I never did learn to sight read music – although I tried hard to acquire the skill. I just could not pitch notes merely by seeing them on a stave. However, I could read time, rhythm and the 'style markings' from a score.

Chapter thirteen

Nerves and a nag

I was always very nervous before performing. I was nervous before I left my house to go to the performance. After lunch, I was even more nervous. But I lost all my nervousness as I walked up the steps to my dressing room. I used to open up my make-up box and start putting on the paint – and, at that moment, all nerves were forgotten. They only came back – slightly – just before I made my first entrance onto the stage.

As I put on my make-up, I always did a few gentle exercises to warm up the voice. I might try one or two notes 'full voice' – such as a top A or even top C to make sure that the 'top' of my voice was in place – but that was all I did. Other singers – notably Elizabeth Schwarzkopf, who was a great singer and a very beautiful lady – made a habit of singing through her part, scene by scene, in full voice before she went on, in order to ensure that her voice was up to singing the next scene. Consequently, in effect, she sang her part twice at every one of her performances! Geraint Evans indulged in this practice too – but I did not. In any case, I never had a problem in being able to finish every performance I began – so my regime worked for me!

Four times, I 'saved the curtain' at the Opera House.

The first occasion was during one performance of Carmen – early on in my career at the Opera House - when Frank Sale broke down and

I had to go to from my home to Covent Garden to sing the rest of the role of Don Jose. Frank was a lovely man – with one really marvellous note in his voice: a top A.

The Daily Graphic (3rd November 1950) either records this incident slightly differently – or chronicles a similar incident. According to the newspaper report: 'Opera singer Edgar Evans answered the telephone from the fireside of his home at Pinner, Middlesex, last night. Thirty minutes later he was singing the principal tenor part in Act III of Carmen at Covent Garden.

James Johnston, who was singing the role of Don Jose in the first and second acts was suffering from an inflamed throat and during Act II it was feared that he might injure his throat if he finished the performance.

So a telephone SOS went out to Edgar Evans who sang the part last year.

His costume was ready for him when he arrived.'

The second occasion was during a performance of The Flying Dutchman. About a week after I had begun to cover the part of Erik, the tenor singing the role was taken ill. So Karl Rankl asked me to sing the role instead. This time – unlike the role of Dancairo in Carmen – it was a tenor role, so I could not refuse!

Entering the stage, the first thing that Erik sings is the word 'Senta' – on a top A. That night, members of the chorus told me that I had sung the word on a top C, perhaps because I was nervous. I don't know about that. I think I sang a top A but I was happy for the members of the chorus to be impressed with my 'top C'.

I was called from home – about 8pm - to take over from the Icelandic tenor Thorstienn Hannesson, when he broke his leg while singing the role of Dmitri in Boris Godunov. He had been brought in to sing the role while I learnt the part of Hermann in The Queen of Spades (more of that later). However, during one evening's performance, he broke his leg while escaping from pursuit by jumping out of a window in the tavern.

As I arrived at the opera house, Thorstienn was being taken away on a stretcher. I went on and sang the role in Dmitri in the 'Polish scenes', which are among the most difficult in the opera.

The News Chronicle reported the incident thus: 'Tenor Edgar Evans clipped seven minutes off his record from his home in Harrow to Covent Garden last night.

Thorstienn Hannesson broke his leg when, playing Dmitri, he made his jump through the window at the climax of the Inn scene in Boris Godunov.

A phone call asked Mr Evans to deputise. He reached Covent Garden by car in 25 minutes. The interval was extended ten minutes and he entered as Dmitri in the next scene.

His previous record – 32 minutes – was set up on 2nd November when the Irish tenor James Johnston, had to give up his part of Don Jose in 'Carmen' after the first act because of chest trouble.'

The final time when I saved the curtain was in February 1960, when Ronald Dowd failed to sing Walther's Prize Song in Die Meistersinger and I had to go on stage in my Vogelgesang costume to sing

● *As Dmitri in Boris Godunov, with Constance Shacklock as Marina.*

the aria. Earlier that evening, David Webster had visited me in my dressing room to ask me to sing Prize Song because Ronald Dowd was not sure if he could finish the performance. I replied that I was not even responsible for covering the part – that was Raymond Nilsson's job.

"I know," replied David, "but we can't find him anywhere."

Incidentally, his 'inability to be found' was the end of Raymond Nilsson as a principal tenor at Covent Garden.

"I still don't know the part," I said.

"But you must have heard it!"

"That's completely different from knowing the part," I replied.

In the end, I agreed to sing just the Prize Song. I remembered that, at a previous performance, Peter Anders – who had been singing the part of Walther – had started singing the Prize Song too early. Consequently, that night I waited for the orchestra to play the opening 'motif' twice, not once - as Anders had done.

Norman Feasey, in the prompt box, mouthed the words to me as my turn came to sing. I was concentrating hard on getting the music right and, with all that was going on, I wasn't going to be able to lip read. So, in a passage where it was just the orchestra playing, I asked Norman – in a stage whisper – to speak the words to me as a prompt, which he did and all passed off well.

There had been no rehearsal. So the first time I ever sang the Prize Song, it was 'for real', in performance, on the stage of the Royal Opera House.

Clive Barnes, writing in The Daily Express (20th February 1960) reported: 'Wagner's Mastersingers – the composer's only comedy – degrenerated into a somewhat grisly farce at Covent Garden last night. Two tenors sang the young Knight, Walther.

The Australian tenor Ronald Dowd, from Sadler's Wells, started under the most taxing, senseless difficulties and won my personal prize for gallantry.

This Covent Garden debut could not have been less auspicious. Suffering from tracheitis – a form of laryngitis – his voice kept on disappearing in the first act.

By the second it had been reduced to a brave but pitiful croak. He could barely speak, let alone sing.

He carried on until the final scene, when the situation became so ludicrous that his place had to be taken – at moments' notice - by Edgar Evans...

To my mind Mr Dowd should not have been permitted to appear. I understand that his understudy – fellow Australian Raymond Nilsson – also had laryngitis...'

In 'The Quiet Showman', the biography of David Webster by Montague Haltrecht (published by Collins, 1975), the story is told that: 'Arthur Carron, who had been reluctant to commit himself at first, had been engaged finally for Trovatore. He could not manage the top note of the 'Miserere', so while Carron as Manrico stood at the small window of the tower in which he is imprisoned, Edgar Evans stood beside him, out of sight, to sing the note for him. But at the last performance in the series, Webster urged Carron to risk failure and sing the note himself.

'"I will," Carron agreed, "but only if Edgar is there next to me."

'Edgar Evans clasped his hand firmly, and Carron managed the note.'

Arthur Carron lived in Swindon and – like me – had been a milkman. He had a marvellous voice and came to Sadler's Wells to sing the role of Otello in 1937 or '38. After that, he went to sing – with great success - at the Metropolitan Opera in New York and at the Colon Opera House in Argentina. He came back to the UK to sing Manrico at Covent Garden at short notice – and it's true that he would only sing in the 'Miserere' scene if I stood by and held his hand. As he approached the top note, he would squeeze my hand and that was my cue to take over for the top notes.

Arthur was a very big man – and as kind as he was large. After my help in those Miserere scenes, he bought my young son, Huw, a 'Junero' building set, which gave Huw many hours of playtime pleasure.

Of course, opportunities to 'save the performance' didn't just come at the Opera House. In December 1953, I was asked to go to Halifax at very short notice to take over from Jimmy Johnston at a Christmas concert – held in the Victoria Hall, Halifax and attended by some 1,200 people.

The subsequent report in the Yorkshire Observer and the Bradford Telegraph & Argus (24th December 1953)

● *Edgar and Nan's son, Huw.*

stated: 'Edgar Evans, at 39 one of the leading tenors in the country, answered a Halifax emergency call last night.

At less than 24 hours notice he deputised for his Covent Garden Opera Company colleague James Johnston, who was prevented by a sudden cold from appearing at the Christmas anniversary concert organised by the firm of John Crossley & Sons Ltd.

Mr Evans, who has taken opera to thousands of homes through the medium of TV and who recently returned from a Wagnerian season with Rome Opera said: "I got a call from the concert agents around midnight. I had no engagement so I readily agreed to stand in."

Mr Evans shared last night's concert platform with soprano Miss Gwen Catley, accompanist Mr Shackleton Pollard and Crossley's Carpet Works Band.'

Subsequently, in the New Year, I deputised for Jimmy Johnston at the Opera House – as Calaf in Turandot and Don Jose in Carmen, while he recovered from his cold.

My career at the Opera House fell into four phases: 1946 to 1955 as I established my name and operatic career; 1955 to 1960 when, despite my illness (in 1955), the Opera House seemed to give me too much to do but, nonetheless, my voice did not feel quite the same as it had been in my earlier days; 1960 to 1969, dominated by the Benjamin Britten operas, and 1969 to 1975, the twilight of my operatic career.

From 1955, I seemed to be 'on' all the time at the Royal Opera House. There seemed to be no end to it. Even in 1954, there were signs – which I did not heed – that my workload was reaching 'overload'.

The Daily Sketch (15th January 1954) reported: 'The big parts in four operas in three days at Covent Garden, London – that will be the singing marathon Mr Edgar Evans, Welsh tenor, will have completed by tonight. Then he has a Leeds concert. It reads like an opera star's nightmare.'

● *As Calaf in Turandot.*

On the Tuesday morning I had sung Calaf in a dress rehearsal of Turandot. That evening, I sang Don Jose in Carmen. On Wednesday evening, I sang the role of Calaf in the performance of Turandot – and again on Thursday when the opera was repeated.

There was even a notice that, 'for the forthcoming (1951/52) season', I would be singing in the Sicilian Vespers with Maria Callas and Boris Christoff – but it never happened, perhaps because Callas couldn't fit it in to her schedule.

Then came the chances to do some recordings – notably Britten's 'Albert Herring' in 1964. Whenever I sang in 'Albert Herring', I sang the part of the Mayor.

In The Tatler, dated 30th December 1959, there's a picture of me, in Boris Gudonov, on horseback. The story that The Tatler doesn't tell is that, on the first night of this production of Boris Gudonov (conducted by Karl Rankl; production by Peter Brook), the horse did not cope well with being on stage during a noisy scene.

The horse was a 'special' horse which had, allegedly, been ridden by 'royalty'. I think his name was 'Winston'. Anyway, I rode this horse onto the stage for the revolution scene but it was very uneasy about the whole thing. It stamped about and generally made a noise. Then Margaret Lane – one of the members of the chorus – gave it a smack with her stick. The horse reared up and set off for the footlights. I managed to turn the horse around but I finished singing at the back of the stage, facing away from the audience!

Brian Godfrey – a member of the

● *On horseback in The Tatler, 1959.*

chorus at the Hoffnung Interplanetary Music Festivals in which Edgar Evans sang, in 1958 and 1959 (see Appendix Two) – has a complementary recollection of the event: "Edgar Evans sang the Pretender in the Covent Garden Boris Godunov, and I remember him coming in on a horse in the Kromy Forest scene. Unfortunately, the horse misbehaved itself. There then followed a strange sound, which was of 2,000 people desperately trying not to laugh!"

The horse was 'retired' for the next performance of the opera, and I made my entrance – and exit – on foot.

Winston was the second horse to be tried in the part and found wanting.

A contemporary newspaper clipping – from an unnamed but probably Welsh newspaper – states: 'Co-incident with the opening of opera week in Ystradgynlais was the opening performance of Boris Gudonov at Covent Garden, London but, unlike Ystradgynlais, Covent Garden had to dispose with the services of one performer who suffered from 'nerves'.

The last act of Boris Gudonov features a revolution and a horse. The tenor, Edgar Evans, has to make an appearance mounted. The first mount chosen was Kate, the black Metropolitan Police mare, ridden by Princess Elizabeth at the Trooping of the Colour last year. She was brought to the theatre daily last week but would not go in – a clear case of 'leading a horse to the water…' – and Kate got the sack.

A new steed was sought and found and – it was hoped would prove to be hard-bitten and seasoned so that Boris should not be let down.'

Unfortunately, Kate's replacement was only able to keep his nerve until he got on stage. Subsequently, there were other horses – including a white horse which David Niven had rode in his film of Bonnie Prince Charlie and an eight year old called Waterford – and I rode them for the rest of the performances. However, even David Niven's former mount was noisy – so noisy in fact that Boris Christoff, who was one of the singers who was singing the part of Boris during the run of performances, greatly objected. In the end, they made the horse rubber shoes to go over his metal ones and put down a huge coconut mat on the stage for him to walk on. That cut the noise down to levels that were acceptable for Boris Christoff – and, presumably, the other Borises in the run: Paulo Silveri, Nicolai Ghiourov and

Marian Nowakowski.

The critics were fulsome in praise of my singing but the horse received mixed reviews.

However, Philip Hope-Wallace, writing in 'Time and Tide' (22nd May 1948), commented: 'Edgar Evans as the Pretender (in Boris Godunov) sang well – it is fun to see a tenor on a horse. I can think of no other opera, except Tchaikovsky's Mazeppa where this happens.'

Peter Wolfe, in 'What's On' (21st May 1948), wrote: '(In Boris Godunov)...there is fine work from Constance Shacklock, Howell Glynne, Richard Lewis and Edgar Evans. The latter is the most satisfactory tenor I've heard at Covent Garden since the Vienna were there. He sings well even on the tired-looking white horse which (the producer, Peter) Brook mistakenly introduces into the last scene.'

● *David Niven's horse meets the cast of Boris Godunov at Covent Garden.*

Chapter fourteen

Grimes and gaffes

I first met Benjamin Britten at Covent Garden and my first association with his operas was singing the role of Peter Grimes – in a performance conducted by Reginald Goodall. It was only later that Ben conducted the work. Of course, Peter Pears had been the first Peter Grimes at Covent Garden but I was the second (around 1948/49).

Subsequently, I did a lot of work with Ben, including recording the part of the Mayor of Loxford in Albert Herring with him (at the Jubilee Hall in Aldeburgh, in April 1964). We rehearsed for the recording in the Red House, which was Ben's house at Aldeburgh.

I had travelled to Aldeburgh in my car, with John Noble (baritone), Harold Blackburn (bass) and Monica Sinclair as the passengers. Monica Sinclair had a well developed sense of humour – and was never far from bursting into laughter. On the way, we went through our parts in the opera - and Harold was particularly amusing because he kept substituting 'naughty' words for the 'real' ones. In addition to making the recording there, we also gave some live performances of Albert Herring at Aldeburgh and, before one of these – with Meredith Davies conducting – I found Harold Blackburn looking very serious indeed in a corner. I asked him: "Are you OK?"

"I have a fear," said Harold.

"Of what?"

"That I might sing those words!"

Even with that danger hanging over us, we all still felt that it was important to have a bit of fun when we performed in these contemporary operas.

Theodore Upman, who was the first to sing Billy Budd at Covent Garden, died recently (March 2005) aged in his 80s. I was the second person – after Peter Pears - to sing Captain Vere in Billy Budd at the Opera House.

I was told that, when – in the 1950s – Billy Budd was put on in Paris, half the audience walked out in protest at the scene where Captain Vere and his lieutenants, Messrs Radcliffe and Redburn, sing: 'We don't like the French and their hoppity skippity ways...'

We were doing a couple of performances of Billy Budd under the baton of Georg Solti. Despite us singers knowing the opera exceptionally well, Solti was new to the opera and so he insisted on some extra rehearsals for us all.

Travelling to Covent Garden on the train (from Preston Road), I thought how much the rhythm of the train, as it went over the track, sounded like the rhythm of the drums in one of the opera's scenes when Captain Vere and his crew are on deck.

At the rehearsal, bored at having to keep doing a part I knew so well, I changed some words in the 'deck scene'. Captain Vere is supposed to sing: "I don't like the look of the mist, Mr Redburn."

This time, I sang: "I don't like the look of your prick, Mr Redburn."

Taken aback, John Shaw, an Australian baritone, as Mr Redburn, had no time to do anything other than reply with the 'correct' response: "No more do I, sir. It may lift but not for long."

The ad lib made the other singers snigger.

When we took Peter Grimes to Wiesbaden (in May 1954), I sang all the performances, while Joan Cross and Sylvia Fisher shared the part of Ellen Orford. After the first night of Peter Grimes, the audience was so enthusiastic that they wouldn't leave the theatre. The theatre management dropped the curtain – but the audience continued clapping and calling. Eventually, they dropped the fire curtain in a vain attempt to get the audience to leave. Finally, the director of the theatre – a Herr Schramm – came to the stage and opened a door so that I could go out to face the audience.

That evening, I got 21 curtain calls. Indeed, all the performances went well. I was amazed at the enthusiasm of the German audience for a contemporary English opera, sung in English. But the house was full each night.

The other remarkable thing about Wiesbaden was the enormous number of nightingales who sang just outside my bedroom window each night. I've never heard so many nightingales in my life! These birds are quite rare in the UK – but there were lots of them in Wiesbaden.

After the first performance of Peter Grimes, we all attended a reception given in our honour by the head of

● *Arriving in Wiesbaden.*

the province that contained Wiesbaden. During the reception, this man's daughter was very attentive to me – flirting openly. Some while later, she even invited me to her wedding!

David Webster – the administrator of the Royal Opera – was with us on the tour, although he left a day or so early. After our last performance in Wiesbaden, Herr Schramm confided in me that David Webster had left without paying his hotel bill – so the Wiesbaden theatre had to pay it!

In my time at Covent Garden, only four tenors sang the part of Grimes: Peter Pears, myself, Richard Lewis and Jon Vickers. Indeed, I sang the part of Peter Grimes before I sang Bob Boles in the same opera.

Raymond Nilsson used to sing Bob Boles and, indeed, sang on the recording of the opera under Benjamin Britten's baton. However, afterwards, Ben said to me: "I wish I'd taken you on to do Bob Boles."

That was probably because Bob Boles is a bit of a 'preacher' and my singing style suited that sort of presentation style.

In my opinion, Jon Vickers was not suited to singing the part of Peter Grimes. He had a very big voice – and it was too big for that part. Moreover, Vickers was a committed Christian and he insisted on changing Grimes' words in the scene towards the end of the opera where Grimes and his apprentice were going out fishing on the sea. Grimes sings: 'Come boy, the whole sea's boiling... Trousers on, coat on...'

Vickers objected to the homosexual undertones contained in these words, so he always changed them when he sang them. I wonder what Ben thought of that!

Being a heterosexual, I wasn't involved in the homosexual side of Ben's character and behaviour. While I was with him, he never showed any glimmer of his sexual preferences. Indeed, although I worked closely with them professionally, I never believed that Ben and Peter could be homosexual lovers. They never openly disclosed their affection for each other when they were in public – especially when they were working together.

● *Rehearsing with Benjamin Britten and Tyrone Guthrie (seated). Peter Gellhorn is on the phone.*

● *Edgar as Bob Boles.*

Chapter fifteen

Dr Sargent and Mr Evans

Sir Malcolm Sargent – always known as 'Dr Sargent' in the north of England – was not my favourite conductor. Mine was a view shared by a number of other singers, including Jess Walters. However, Sir Malcolm championed Richard Lewis. He liked him because Richard was an excellent sight reader and so needed little or no rehearsal.

My agents, Ibbs & Tillett, once called me to ask me to sing in The Seasons with Sir Malcolm Sargent in Liverpool. I said to them: "No. I don't want to sing with Sargent and I wouldn't dream of going to Liverpool to perform with him."

I didn't get asked again.

Previously, I had done two Messiahs with Sir Malcolm Sargent – both in the Potteries area of England. Both of these performances were before I had gone to Covent Garden. Indeed, I was in Gay Rosalinda at the time.

I had never sung The Messiah before – although I had learnt the part on the offchance that I might be asked to sing it – and then my first ever performance of the work was with Sir Malcolm Sargent, one of the acclaimed authorities on the work.

I had learnt my part in The Messiah with the appoggiaturas but Sir Malcolm insisted in me cutting them out. I tried my best – but I daresay the odd one or two crept in, unbidden, in performance.

I didn't sing many oratorios. Apart the Messiahs I sang with Sir Malcolm Sargent, I sang in Elijah but I never sang in other sacred music such as requiems – although I did learn the Verdi Requiem just in case an offer came!

There was a man called Harry who was crazy about singing and was known as 'the Hans Sachs of the North' because of it. He might also have been in the shoe trade – which also would have strengthened the allusion. He had been at some of the concerts I had given during the War and, when I got a call from Ibbs & Tillett saying that 'Harry' wanted me to sing in The Messiah, I thought it must be this 'Harry' – especially since he was from the north of England and The Messiah was very popular there.

It was only later that I found out that 'Harry' was a nickname for Sir Malcolm Sargent – because musicians used to call him 'Flash Harry' because of his dress sense.

That frightened me a bit – not because I didn't know the part (I knew it very well) but because I knew, from other singers, of Sir Malcolm's reputation for being a bit 'schoolmastery'.

In rehearsal, when I came to sing 'Thy rebuke has broken his heart...', I was astonished. He took the piece at a fast tempo, allowing no expression, meaning or emotion in the singing at all. I tried to object but Sir Malcolm said: "You'll do it as I conduct it."

This was typical of the man. I couldn't find in him any 'feeling' for the music he was conducting. He came to prominence – especially in the north, where they adored him – because of his ability to work with choirs.

Later, I met a pianist – called Joseph Green, who came from Liverpool – who also confessed that he had had a 'run in' with Sir Malcolm Sargent over timing.

When it came to the second Messiah, I knew what to expect.

On both occasions, I sang with Isobel Baillie and Kathleen Ferrier. The bass in the first performance was Robert Easton and, in the second, it was Owen Brannigan.

I was booked to sing the part of Bacchus, the god of wine, in The Olympians, by Arthur Bliss, at the Royal Albert Hall – with Sir Malcolm Sargent conducting. In the concert, I was also due to sing

'Celeste Aida', take part in the grand scene from Aida, as well as singing in the quintet from Die Mastersinger von Nürnberg. I was deputising for the tenor Walter Midgeley, who was also not keen to sing under Sargent's baton and had become 'indisposed'.

About three days before the concert, Sir Malcolm called everyone involved in the performance – soloists and chorus – to a rehearsal at the Royal College of Music. During this rehearsal, I heard my cue to sing – so I began singing. Sir Malcolm stopped proceedings and said to me: "I don't want you to sing. I'm working with the chorus."

Later on, I heard another of my cues and so, again, began to sing – only to be told the same thing by Sir Malcolm.

The rehearsal ended – and not one of the principals had been asked to sing, although we had all been there throughout the rehearsal.

The next day, I heard from Joan Ingpen, of my then agents, Ingpen & Williams, that Jimmy Johnston could not now sing the part of Hoffmann in The Tales of Hoffmann in Dublin. Peter Gellhorn had asked Joan to ask me to go to Dublin and sing the part instead. Obviously, I went to Dublin to sing Hoffmann – so I couldn't be at the final rehearsal for the Albert Hall concert. Consequently, Sir Malcolm then had no chance to hear me sing before the actual performance.

As it happened, the performance was fine – except that Sir Malcolm gave me a 'lead' that he should have given to Jess Walters. At the interval, Sir Malcolm asked me why I had not sung when he had given me the cue. I explained that, if I had sung then, he would not have heard what he had expected to hear.

In my experience of him, Sir Malcolm Sargent was a competent conductor but he was out of his depth when it came to conducting grand opera.

As conductors, Sir Malcolm Sargent and Sir Thomas Beecham were poles apart where bringing out the 'feeling' of the piece was concerned – although both were sticklers for 'doing it their way'. Indeed, there is a story told that, when Sir Thomas took over conducting an orchestra that had previously been conducted by Sir Malcolm, he began by addressing the orchestra members with the words: "Is this the Sargent's mess?"

There were two, Scottish brothers – William Dickie, who was a baritone, and Murray Dickie, who was a tenor. Murray, who later went on to be one of the main tenors at the Vienna State Opera, was rehearsing the part of David in Die Mastersinger von Nürnberg at Covent Garden – with Sir Thomas Beecham.

During the opera, David has a song with the apprentices and they were rehearsing this part of the opera. Murray – as David – made a mistake and Sir Thomas asked him to do it again. He did, but made the same mistake. Instantly, Sir Thomas bellowed: "Senior repetiteur! Take this man away and teach him his part!"

When Sir Thomas Beecham was asked to return to Covent Garden after the War to conduct Die Mastersinger von Nürnberg, he wanted to hear every 'master' soloist sing his or her part individually. All the singers duly arrived on stage and Beecham shouted: Let's hear the first master."

So, as Vogelgesang, the first master, I had to begin.

I sang my whole part – straight through but bit by bit, as it occurred throughout the score. Before long, Sir Thomas became tired of this and shouted: "You're OK."

Then, realising how tedious this process was going to be – especially for him – he dismissed the cast.

I was pleased with this because I had another appointment to go to: to rehearse the part of des Grieux in Manon with Victoria de los Angeles, who had just arrived in the UK to make her first appearance at Covent Garden.

● *Rehearsing with Victoria de los Angeles. Warwick Braithwaite is the conductor, with Monia Young at the piano.*

Chapter sixteen

Crits and compliments

I only ever had one bad 'crit'. It was printed in a local (not national) paper and came about because the reviewer had been captivated by Victoria de los Angeles in Manon. Enamoured of her, he had written of me: 'Who is this creature?'

I got a barrister friend of mine to write to the paper – and they printed the following apology: 'In this column certain statements were made on 14th June (1951) concerning a performance of Mr Edgar Evans at Covent Garden in the opera Manon. It has now been suggested to the Editor of this paper and to the writer of this column that these statements went beyond the limit of fair criticism of him as an opera singer and were derogatory to a man of his reputation. Since these statements are capable of such an interpretation we publicly apologise to Mr Edgar Evans. In making this apology we wish to make it clear that we hope and indeed feel sure that his high reputation as a singer has in no way been impaired by what was said.' (Montague Calman's Show Topics, The Kentish Observer, 16th August 1951)

I always read the crits because I believe that it's important to read what people think about what you've done. It gives you an opportunity to correct yourself and, if there's something in a crit that can help you – even if it's a less favourable report than you'd hoped -

then it's a good thing to have read.

I've had many more positive comments on my singing - and acting. And Joan Ayling, the famous painter of miniatures and the wife of a Harley Street gynaecologist, painted my picture twice – once in my Captain Vere costume from Billy Budd. She wouldn't take any money for the paintings and gave them to me as a sign of her appreciation for my work.

According to Gladys Davidson in 'Opera Biographies', (1955): 'Among the important roles [Edgar Evans] has sung at Covent Garden, in addition to that of des Grieux in Manon, are: Don Jose in Carmen, Alfredo in La Traviata, Riccardo in A Masked Ball, Rudolfo in La Boheme, Hermann in The Queen of Spades, Dmitri in Boris Godunov, Erik in The Flying Dutchman, Narraboth in Salome, Florestan in Fidelio, Turiddu in Cavalleria Rusticana, Andres in Wozzeck, Captain Vere in Billy Budd, Prince Calaf in Turandot. In the latter he gives a remarkably virile and romantic, yet mentally alert performance. This is considered by many as one of his best parts. It provides, too, a particularly interesting contrast from his own entirely original and clever rendering of the difficult, psychological role of Captin Vere in Benjamin Britten's tense opera, Billy Budd.

I was singing Zinovy in the premiere at Covent Garden of Shostakovich's opera Katerina Ismailova. We had finished the dress rehearsal and, since my character

● *Edgar as Zinovy in Katerina Ismailova.*

is not present in the last scene of the opera, I'd asked permission – and been granted it – to go and get changed early. Then, on the tannoy, there was a message for me to return to the stage. There, I met Shostakovich. He couldn't speak any English but he had an interpreter with him.

Shostakovich said something to me in Russian. I turned to the interpreter. She said: "Mr Shostakovich says that you are the best Zinovy that he has ever heard – or seen acted."

I felt that was quite a compliment!

I was also in the Covent Garden premiere of Ralph Vaughan Williams' Pilgrim's Progress – singing two parts: The Interpreter and A Celestial Messenger. It was an opera that David Webster didn't like at all! However, it gave me the chance to meet Vaughan Williams. He was very appreciative of all our efforts and I thought him a very kind man. I liked him very much.

According to Hubert Foss, writing in The Musical Times (of June 1951): 'Edgar Evans, as the Interpreter and later as the Heavenly Messenger, took the stage by singing and deportment better than that of the rest of the company.'

● *Carlo Maria Giulini.*

The Irish Times (30th April 1951) commented: 'The best singing was that of Edgar Evans as interpreter at the House Beautiful.'

When Don Carlos was to performed at Covent Garden in 1958, the conductor was to be Carlo Maria Giulini and the producer was the legendary film-maker, Luchino Visconti.

I was told that I was to sing the part of the Count of Lerma, a Spanish nobleman. However, the part is very small – no more than a few lines at the beginning and later on in the opera. Since I had been singing larger parts at the Opera House – especially since creating the part of Hermann in The Queen of Spades, under Kleiber – I said that I did not want to do the part because it was too small.

So I was sent to see David Webster, the administrator. He told me that Giulini and Visconti were very keen for me to do the part and that I should go and talk to them about it. So I went to the

● *Edgar as Count Lerma in Don Carlos.*

● *Rehearsing Pilgrim's Progress with Ralph Vaughan Williams.*

● *With Vaughan Williams, Adele Leigh and Iris Kells.*

71

conductor's room – Room 'A' – and saw them. I told them that Lerma was not an important part in the opera.

"But," they said, "Lerma is important. He is to be the next ruler of Spain."

"Then I'll do the part when Lerma is ruler of Spain," I replied.

Then Visconti said: "Who else can we have to do the part?"

"There are plenty of others about," I said.

"But none of them are as tall as you. Lerma has to be an imposing, aristocratic figure – which you are just right to play the part."

I still said that I didn't want to do the part but, later, I met David Webster. He said: "They want you to do the part. You'd better do it."

Faced with that that sort of veiled ultimatum – the sort that hints that if you don't do what you're being asked, you're not going to stay with the company for long – I swallowed my pride and did the part.

I've never been completely satisfied with any performance I've given – except on one night: a performance of A Masked Ball in 1953 – singing with Tito Gobbi. Hearing Gobbi reminded me of Ricci's

● *At the end of A Masked Ball with Jess Walters, Adele Leigh and Helena Verte.*

teaching – since Ricci had been Gobbi's teacher as well as mine. It inspired me to sing the best I ever sang.

The resulting crit said: 'As the cheerful but unfortunate King of Sweden (in Masked Ball), Edgar Evans follows in the line of some of the greatest tenors who have ever sung in opera, including Jean de Reske and Caruso.' (Education, November 27, 1953)

Rehearsing one day for La Traviata, I was on stage when I noticed the telephone ring in the stage manager's box. The stage manager came over to me.

"I've got a call for you from Walter Legge. He wants you to go now to sing Melot in a recording of Tristan und Isolde."

"But I'm rehearsing the part of Alfredo here."

"Don't worry about that. Go and do the recording," he said.

So I went. I was introduced to the conductor, Wilhelm Furtwängler, and we went through the part of Melot.

"Good," said Furtwängler and we recorded the part within the day.

I was delighted to have been asked to be on the recording – although Furtwängler was reputed to have been unhappy at the quality of the sound on the recording. The recording featured some great singers, including Dietrich Fischer-Dieskau and Kirsten Flagstadt. It also featured the Top C of Elizabeth Schwarzkopf, who sang it on behalf of Flagstadt. This was well known among those in the singing profession but was kept from the opera buying public.

In my very early days at Covent Garden, I sang the role of the young seaman in Tristan und Isolde. The seaman sings unaccompanied but shares his two final notes with Isolde – who was being played by Kirsten Flagstadt. Afterwards, the conductor, John Gardner, remarked to me that I hadn't been at Covent Garden very long but already I had sung a duet with the world's greatest opera singer!

Of even more value to me was that the internationally known bass, Marian Nowakowski often used to pay me the immensely pleasing compliment of saying: "Edgar, you sound just like Caruso."

● *Edgar as Melot in Tristan und Isolde.*

Chapter seventeen

Teachers and Turandot

Soon after the War, Joseph (Joe) Hislop was engaged by The Royal Opera to teach its young singers – such as Rhydderch Davies and me. He was a charming man and was always telling jokes. He had one or two useful ideas – such as getting us to learn short songs or 'aria antiquae', such as 'Amaryllis' in order to develop a 'line' in our singing. However, he didn't have anything to teach about technique – and I really wanted him to teach technique. Technique in singing is vital. If you don't have – and develop – it you will never have the vocal stamina and ability to sing strenuous roles continuously.

So, unfortunately, I didn't learn much from Joe Hislop. However, at the last rehearsal for Tchaikovsky's opera The Queen of Spades, in which I sang the role of Hermann (see chapter 20), Joe came to see me back stage and said: "Edgar, you will mention me as your teacher won't you?"

I smiled but I didn't reply.

However, the story of Joe Hislop being Edgar Evans' vocal coach must have got about because, writing in 'Opera Biographies' (1955), Gladys Davidson records: '[Edgar Evans] continued his vocal studies, this time with Mr Joseph Hislop, with whom he worked throughout 1948 and 1949 and during which period he also appeared frequently at Covent Garden in many principal tenor roles, as well as in various lesser parts from time to time.'

It was Erich Kleiber's idea that I should go to study in Vienna with the English tenor Alfred Picaver, who had made a great name for himself throughout Europe. Unfortunately, Picaver was ill and so, instead, Kleiber suggested – and the Royal Opera agreed – to send me to Rome in 1950, to study under the great teacher, Ricci, who was in his 60s when I met him.

It was so that I could learn the part of the king in Masked Ball that Covent Garden sent me to Ricci. Ricci taught me to sing the aria in the opera in which the king laughs at the woman who has cursed him by laughing to the music throughout the opening lines of the aria, rather than singing the 'set' words. When I got back to London and started rehearsing this aria, the conductor - John Pritchard – could not believe that this was 'how they did things in Rome'.

John Pritchard conducted Verdi's Masked Ball when I sang in the opera's premiere at Covent Garden after the War. In that premiere season I sang five performances of the opera – each one with a different Amelia.

● *Edgar as Riccardo in A Masked Ball.*

The first was Helena Verte, but she became ill before the second performance and another singer took her place. The next one in the role was Joan Sutherland and she was superseded by the Dutch soprano, Gré Brouwenstijn. All of them, with the possible exception of Joan Sutherland, became ill – as, indeed, did Jess Walters, who was also taking a major role (of Renato) in the production. Even I was so unwell during that run that twice I cancelled my final aria in the opera!

The part of the king in Masked Ball is the hardest – most vocally taxing - part I ever sang. Ultimately, I don't think that I was a 'Verdi tenor'. I could sing roles in Puccini's operas but the Verdi tenor parts call for a 'heavier' sound than I really possessed.

Boris Christoff, the world renowned bass, did not have a big voice. However, he produced his voice beautifully, always giving sense to what he was singing.

I felt that my voice was like that. Because I couldn't sight read music, I had to work hard, with the help of a piano - before even rehearsing a piece – to learn not only the words and music but also to make sense of what I was singing and express the emotion of the music.

Kleiber and Barbirolli recognised this. Indeed, Sir John Barbirolli ensured that I sang the role of Calaf in all the performances of Turandot that he conducted at Covent Garden.

After I came back from Rome, David Webster wanted to know how I had got on there – because the Royal Opera paid for me to be there for six weeks, having a half hour lesson with Ricci each day (I paid for everything else on the trip – including buying a car (a Railton drop-head coupe, for £400), in which I drove Nan, Huw (then aged eight) and myself all the way there and back!).

I said that I had got on quite well with Ricci but I would like to go to see him once more.

"However," I said, "I can now sing a top 'C' any time you like."

● *Edgar's first car - a Railton drop head coupe, one of only 24 ever made.*

David Webster picked up the telephone on his desk and spoke into it.

"Is John (Barbirolli) there?" he said. "John, I've got Edgar Evans here. He says he can sing a top 'C' any time he likes."

David Webster looked at me and said: "Will you go to the Foyer (of the Royal Opera House) and sing for him?"

Sir John Barbirolli was rehearsing some performers in the Foyer – and I went to see him. I didn't have any music with me that contained a top 'C' so, instead, I sang 'Nessun Dorma', from Turandot, which has a top 'B flat'. Within three weeks, I was singing Calaf at the Royal Opera House, under the baton of John Barbirolli. Later, I sang the role on tour, again with Barbirolli conducting.

While I was with the Royal Opera, I also was sent to study in

Munich (in September 1963). Georg Solti sent me there to learn the part of Lohengrin from Solti's 'right hand man' when he had been in Hamburg: Dr Hallasch. I learnt the part because I was covering a German tenor who was singing Lohengrin at Covent Garden at the time. I always wanted to sing the part – but I never did.

Dr Hallasch told me how dangerous an adversary Solti could be. He told me the story of how Solti had sacked a long-serving baritone in Hamburg only a year before he was eligible for a pension.

At Covent Garden one day, rehearsing Il Trovatore, Forbes Robinson sang the line: "This woman is bewitched."

Solti stopped the rehearsal.

"Sing it properly," he said. "Sing: 'Zis voman is beviched.'"

So Forbes Robinson did exactly as he was told – and then got told off for it!

● *Georg Solti (left) with Dr Hallasch.*

Chapter eighteen

Royal reminiscences

One year, during the 1980s, Prince Charles and Princess Diana attended the Covent Garden Christmas party in the Crush Bar at the opera house. During the party, Prince Charles entertained the gathering by singing a song from one of the Gilbert & Sullivan operas. Afterwards, I met the Prince and said to him: "You're a bit croaky tonight!"

"Ah! Excuse me for that," he replied. "Very recently, I fell off my polo pony and, as I landed, my stick caught my windpipe. What can I do?"

At the time, I was teaching singing at the Royal College of Music but I had no answer for him. In both of my careers – as a singer and a teacher of singing – I had never come across anyone who had been hit on the windpipe by a polo stick!

Nearly 20 years earlier – in 1969 - I had met the Queen at the Opera House when she attended a performance there. After the performance, the Queen said to me: "You're Welsh, aren't you?"

I replied: "Yes. We're all very pleased about the forthcoming Investiture (of Prince Charles as Prince of Wales). I hope it's all going well?"

"Yes, it is," the Queen replied.

Of course, I was hoping to be asked to take part in the Investiture but, in the end, I missed out. The selection of the singers for the

● *Edgar is presented to the Queen on the Royal Opera House's 21st anniversary. In the background (right) is John Tooley.*

Investiture was greatly influenced by my colleague and namesake at the Royal Opera, Geraint Evans. Even so, I was surprised to learn, some weeks later, that Geraint's half brother – who had been at Covent Garden to sing a small part in a production of Billy Budd in which I sang Captain Vere – was chosen to be one of the tenors to sing at the Investiture.

My nephew, Vernon Griffiths, found himself in court shortly before the Investiture of the Prince of Wales in 1969, on charges related to his alleged membership of the 'Free Wales Army'. The first I knew about it was when his solicitor telephoned me, about 4.30pm, to say that he was applying for bail and needed someone to stand bail on Vernon's behalf in the sum of £4,000 – a lot of money in those days!

I said that I could find £2,000 and the solicitor said that that would be alright because a neighbouring farmer – who was named David Evans but was no relation, although he and I had been at school together and we were the best of friends – at Alltgoch Farm, had offered to put up the other £2,000. Incidentally, today, Alltgoch Farm contains a large quarry.

One day – when I was 16 or 17 years old – I was on my way home after having had a haircut from Tom 'Bryn View' when I saw Thomas and John 'Allt Goch' with a spade and a pickaxe by the road. They were digging and I watched them pick up a piece of rock. I asked them what they were doing. They said: "We think this rock is suitable for crushing to help make tarmac, so we're taking this piece to be tested."

The rock passed the test – and that was the beginning of a huge quarry that has been employing a large number of people for many years.

In 1969, though, our combined offer – from 'Mr Evans Alltgoch' and me - of £4,000 bail money was refused because of fears about what might happen at the Prince's Investiture. So the judge kept Vernon and several others in prison until Prince Charles was safely out of the Principality.

I came into contact with members of the Royal family at other times during my career – including Princess Margaret, whom I met one evening at the

● *With Lord Harewood.*

Opera House. We spoke about corgis – since, at the time, we both owned one.

I got on well with Lord Harewood, the Queen's cousin. Before he became the director of English National Opera, Lord Harewood was deputy to David Webster at Covent Garden. Initially, he used 'Room A' at the opera house – which was the conductors' room – until he had his own office. One day, Jimmy Johnston and I had been asked to go to see him. As we stood outside the door of Room A, Jimmy said: "What shall we call him?"

"My lord?" I suggested

"That's too much," said Jimmy. "Do you think we can call him George?"

We were so unsure of protocol that we neatly avoided calling him anything during our subsequent conversation. Later on, Lord Harewood became so much a part of the team at the opera house that, in the end, we all called him 'George'.

One evening, during a Royal Opera tour, we were performing Carmen at the Grand Theatre, Leeds. I was going up to the dressing room and met Lord Harewood and David Webster coming down the stairs.

"How are you?" enquired Lord Harewood.

"I've got a cold. I'm not sure how I'm going to get through the performance," I replied.

"Well, do what Constance Shacklock does: mind over matter!" Lord Harewood said.

Constance was playing Carmen in this production, while I was playing Don Jose. She – like Joyce Grenfell, with whom I had toured during the War – was a Christian Scientist and so did not believe in the power of pain or infirmity. Many years later, Constance died of cancer of the pancreas. True to her beliefs, throughout her illness she did not visit a doctor.

● *Edgar, as Count Lerma (in Don Carlos) meets the Queen Mother at Covent Garden.*

Chapter nineteen

Anecdotes and animosity

A s in any profession, there is some degree of professional jealousy in the musical world. And its sub-set, the world of professional singing, is no exception. This sentiment is recognised in Wales, which has a justifiable reputation as highly musical nation, and has been accorded its own phrase in Welsh - 'cythrel y canu' – which can be translated as the 'devilment in singing'.

Perhaps the existence of jealousy is understandable in a profession so closely connected with the performing arts, where success or failure in a career can be influenced by others' interpretations and actions.

I like to think that I got on well with most people – at least, with as many as possible – during my time as a professional singer. However, there will always be people who are jealous of your position, or who want what you have.

In this context, I always felt uncomfortable about James (Jimmy) Johnston - a tenor who, in addition to working at Covent Garden Opera House, I believe owned a butcher's shop on the Falls Road in Northern Ireland (which he employed a manager to run for him during his singing career).

Jimmy Johnston, Richard Lewis and I were tenors and we all got on well together socially. Indeed, Richard Lewis was a good friend – even if he was happy to undercut me as far as fees were concerned to get work! But Richard and Jimmy always tried to get me out of way or, in some way, get jobs ahead of me. That's the way of life, though, in this profession: there are a number of jobs for baritones and bases but relatively few for tenors - so the competition for those jobs is necessarily keener, even if there are relatively fewer tenors than basses and baritones.

Towards the end of his performing career, Gerald Davies, an excellent tenor, principally known as a soloist at Sadler's Wells and who went on to be a teacher at the Welsh College of Music and Drama, said to me: "I'm going to give up as a singer because it's all 'dog eat dog' here."

While I admired the vocal ability of many baritones and bases – notably Boris Christoff, who had a wonderful voice, full of emotion, that was ideally suited to the roles of Philip of Spain in Don Carlos and Boris in Boris Godunov – I had some heated exchanges with the base, David Franklin, who went on from Covent Garden to make a career in broadcasting as a regular member of the 'My Music' team on BBC Radio 4.

One evening, while singing the role of Dmitri in Boris Godunov, I was doing a scene with David Franklin, who was playing the part of Pimen. During the scene – for dramatic effect – I put my hand on his right arm as I was (singing) asking him a question. During a pause in the singing, as the orchestra was playing, he said to me – sotto voce: "Take your bloody hand off me."

I thought that that was odd. None of the other Pimens in that production had objected to that move of mine. When the scene was over and we were both off stage, I went to see David.

"Why did you say that?" I asked.

● *Edgar as Dmitri in Boris Godunov.*

"There was no need for you to say that!"

It was not a pleasant confrontation. David always thought himself superior to everyone else. Once – in my hearing – he asked Karl Rankl: "Can I call you Karl?"

"No! You call me Mr Rankl," was the sharp retort from a man who had no favourites.

At the beginning of one season at Covent Garden, I had just come out of hospital after having an operation to remove a cyst from my bottom. As I entered the Opera House, David Franklin greeted me with a sarcastic laugh and said, in a loud voice: "Here comes Evans the cyst!"

I thought that was unkind to say the least – especially since David had a medical condition of his own – so I replied: "Glad to see you, 'Dai goitre'!"

After David died, there was some celebration of his life – possibly organised by the BBC, for whom he had worked for some time. I was asked to go along and contribute a story or two about him but I refused. As I said to the organiser: "I don't want to contribute because David behaved atrociously to other artists and to me while he was at Covent Garden. If I come along, I will have to say that."

Naturally, the organiser agreed with me that it was better if I stayed away.

One of the greatest friendships that I forged at the Opera House that later turned, sadly, into some animosity was my relationship with my namesake and fellow principal at the Royal Opera, Geraint – later Sir Geraint – Evans.

Geraint Evans came to Covent Garden not long after I did. He joined the company in the 1947/48 season – and his first part was as the nightwatchman in Die Meistersinger von Nürnberg. Initially, we were great friends – for many years, in fact. However, things turned sour after Geraint had returned from singing the role of Wozzeck in the USA.

I had played the role of Andres in Wozzeck at Covent Garden, working with Marco Rothmuller in the title role. Later, I played the role of the Drum Major, while Jess Walters played Wozzeck. Rothmuller was a friend of the work's composer, Alban Berg – as was Erich Kleiber, the musical director, and the producer, Sumner Austin.

Indeed, Erich Kleiber was an acknowledged expert on this particular opera.

Before the next season's performances of Wozzeck (probably in 1960) Geraint had been to the USA and had performed the work there - I believe it was in San Francisco.

I was getting ready in my dressing room before going to rehearse Wozzeck, when Ken MacDonald looked in. He said: "When you get on the stage you'll find it's all changed! We're not doing it as we did last year because Geraint doesn't like it. So we're doing it his way."

Then Otakar Kraus came up and told us that there was quite an argument going on, on stage, over the production – and Geraint was winning it.

I went to the stage to rehearse the scene in the barracks where I, as the Drum Major, pick on Wozzeck. When I got to the stage, Geraint said to me: "This time, I'm coming out my bed to attack you."

● *Edgar as the Drum Major in Wozzeck.*

"You wouldn't do that!" I said. "A private soldier wouldn't attack a drum major - especially in the German army!"

"Well, that's how it's interpreted in America," he replied.

"We're doing it as we used to do with Kleiber," I said. "I'm not going to do it your way."

"Why not?"

"Because it would make you too strong. Wozzeck is the weak link in this opera. That's what this opera is all about. Everyone takes advantage of Wozzeck – so it's completely out of character for him to attack the Drum Major."

The rehearsal stopped and I went home.

Before supper, as I was telling Nan how Geraint was behaving, the telephone rang. It was Andy Anderson, the stage manager at the opera house.

"Edgar," he said, "we must settle this Drum Major scene. Please come in tomorrow morning for 10.30 and sort it out with Geraint."

The next morning, I arrived on time but Geraint was late. He had been held up in traffic.

I said: "What's the problem about this scene?"

"It's your problem, not mine," said Geraint.

The next thing I knew, Andy Anderson and David Webster appeared. David Webster took me to one side and said: "Look, Edgar, if he wants it that way, it doesn't cost you anything to agree."

I put up a bit of a fight but you couldn't argue with the head of the company. So I did what Geraint wanted and, in the performance, he got out of his bed to attack me, as the Drum Major.

In the resulting 'crit', the reviewer said that, as the Drum Major, I was 'the weakest link'. This was the result of Geraint changing the production!

David Webster had gone to Rome but a few days later, I received a letter from him in which he said that he was sorry that I was described as 'the weakest link' in the production and he told me 'not to worry'. Nonetheless, a crit like that could lose you your contract – or at least sow such seeds in the minds of those in charge of the company.

In the biography of David Webster, 'The Quiet Showman' by Montague Haltrecht (published by Collins, 1975), this incident is dealt with thus: '(Webster) didn't often visit singers in their dressing rooms, nervous that in the emotion of the moment, and on their territory, he'd commit himself to something he'd afterwards regret. He had all the more to be remote because he was emotional and easily moved. But the singers felt noticed. Everybody felt noticed. He only visited Edgar Evans in his dressing room twice in 25 years, but once he wrote to him from Rome, where he was holding auditions, after seeing bad notices in the English papers – "As long as I'm pleased it doesn't matter what they say."'

Before the next performance of Wozzeck – a few days later – I said to Geraint: "You stay in your bed. Don't come out."

In the performance, Geraint went to get out the bed to attack me but I was prepared for it so, as he moved, I reached forward, grabbed him and dragged him out of the bed. As he came out from the bed, I gave him the usual stage business 'shove'.

"You hurt me," said Geraint as the scene continued.

Geraint Evans appears to confirm this in his book, 'A Knight at the Opera' (published in 1984). When dealing with the twilight of his career, he wrote: 'Fate now…sent me tumbling from a ladder at home in Aberaeron a few weeks before I was due to leave for Chicago. I'd broken a rib a couple of times before, playing rugby on one occasion, and even when I was caught off-balance during a fight with Edgar Evans, who was playing the Drum Major (in Wozzeck)…'

Although our great friendship subsequently cooled, I went to Geraint's home town of Cilfynydd, near Pontypridd, to sing when he was invested with the CBE. He was a great artist, even if he was not always the kindest or most unselfish of men.

After I had sung the major role of Hermann in Tchaikovsky's opera The Queen of Spades, the next production was The Magic Flute, in which I usually played the part the First Man in Armour, while Geraint Evans played the Second Man in Armour. We had received some critical acclaim for our efforts in these parts, too.

The Musical Express (9th April 1948) commented: 'The production at Covent Garden of The Magic Flute is infinitely better than that of the 'Valkyrie'. One of the most striking things about it was that in the whole of its long cast there is not a single weak character; the two soldiers (Edgar Evans and Geraint Evans) who appear only for one scene near the end sing their parts with the certainty and quality of principals.'

Since I had sung the role of Hermann, Dr Kleiber wanted me to stop singing the role of the Armed Man in The Magic Flute and concentrate on the larger roles at the Opera House. However, he did not feel the same way about Geraint. Nonetheless, Geraint was highly ambitious and wanted to 'move on' to sing larger parts too. So he asked Dr Kleiber to be excused from singing the Second Man in Armour role.

"Why? Don't you want to sing with me?" asked Kleiber.

"Of course, but I don't think that Edgar and I are suited to those parts," Geraint replied. He had been happy to sing the role with me but was jealous that I had 'moved on' while he had to be paired with another – presumably 'junior' – tenor.

"Let me be the judge of that," said Kleiber. And that was that.

Ron Lewis, a baritone and excellent musician who began working life as a waiter and then was one of the few singers to become a principal singer at the Royal Opera having been promoted from being in the chorus (another was Michael Langdon), always used to say that 'you're nowhere unless you're doing the top part' in an opera. No doubt Geraint would have agreed. Of course, there's nothing wrong in wanting to better yourself – but I think that you shouldn't try to do at others' expense by putting them 'down'.

The production after The Magic Flute, under Kleiber - when Geraint wanted to 'better himself' – was Carmen. I only ever sang the part of Don Jose in Carmen. I never sang any other part in the opera. Indeed, I have sung the part of Don Jose more times that I have sung any other operatic role. I sang it under the batons of Keliber, Reginald Goodall, Ted Downes, John Pritchard and others.

So, as usual, I sang the role of Don Jose, while Geraint was the Escamillo. Geraint was not the best Escamillo ever but, as David Webster, used to remind us: "We're a repertory company, so we can only put on the best we've got!"

In David Webster's biography, 'The Quiet Showman' by Montague Haltrecht (published by Collins, 1975), Haltrecht reports that: 'Webster one day met Geraint Evans walking in the street with his wife and he told him he'd be doing the Torreador in Carmen once more.

"'But he's terrible in the part," Geraint's wife (Brenda) felt bound to point out.

"'Yes," Webster casually drawled. "I suppose he is. But he's the best we've got.'"

One evening, Geraint got into trouble with the producer, Christopher West. At the end of the familiar 'Torreador song' in Carmen, Geraint – as Escamillo, the Torreador – climbed on top of a table, standing out in the opera's 'big' scene. Afterwards, Christopher told Geraint not to stand on the table, drawing attention to himself, but to always stand with the chorus.

On this occasion, however, I agreed with Geraint. Escamillo, with all his daring and bravado, needs to be visible at the end of 'Carmen'.

After all, it's the only aria that Escamillo has – so why not make the most of it?

I believe that the best Escamillo of my time was Denis Noble. Denis had sung in the performance of Manon in which I made my Covent Garden debut. Afterwards, he congratulated me on 'going through with the part' of des Grieux. I understood his point: the part of des Grieux is a hard part – almost as hard as the part of Riccardo in A Masked Ball, but in a different way. Perhaps it's the difference between French and Italian opera – but both these roles are extremely tough, in their own way, to perform.

Also in Montague Haltrecht's biography of David Webster is the passage: 'Singers were also overworked. Edgar Evans who, in the first season, had taken over the role of des Grieux from Heddle Nash, before very long was finding himself called on to undertake sometimes as many as four exacting roles in a single week, ranging perhaps from the heroic tenor Calaf in Turandot to a Britten role. There was nothing Webster could do about it. In the company's first few years if not Walter Midgley or James Johnston for the tenor roles, then it was most likely to be Edgar Evans. It told. In 1955 he was away from the company for 20 weeks, suffering from nervous exhaustion.'

One week, I sang Pinkerton in Madam Butterfly on Monday evening, rehearsed all the week for the part of Peter Grimes, under the baton of Benjamin Britten; then, on Friday evening, I sang Max in Der Freischutz, on Saturday, I was Don Jose in Carmen and on the following Monday, I sang the role of Peter Grimes in performance. After a rehearsal of The Tales of Hoffmann conducted by Reginald Goodall, I collapsed at home. I telephoned the Opera House to say that I could not come to the next rehearsal. However, it was the end of the season and, in the evening, I did the performance – of Hoffmann. When I was singing the final aria, I thought – with all the pressure and stress that I was feeling – that the top of my head was going to fly into the audience.

I was burnt out. I was away from the Opera House from 20 weeks – giving my rivals plenty of opportunities to take on the roles I had been doing. Then, walking with the aid of a stick and supported, too, by my wife, Nan, I went to see David Webster. He simply told me to 'pull myself together'.

● *Edgar, in his debut role of des Grieux in Manon...*

● *Pinkerton in Madam Butterfly...*

● *Max in Der Freischutz...*

● *and Riccardo in A Masked Ball.*

● *At home with his wife, Nan, during his enforced absence from Covent Garden.*

Chapter twenty

Gellhorn and Hermann

Peter Gellhorn was an amazing person and an incredible musician. His knowledge of music - and especially of opera – was beyond anyone else. He knew the lot!

Peter was the first repetiteur at Covent Garden after the War and eventually headed a group of three or four repetiteurs – which included John Gardiner and Eric Mitchell. Eric was Constance Shacklock's husband. One of his jobs at Covent Garden was to play the Opera House organ when it was required – for example, in Manon. Indeed, his introduction to des Grieux's aria, 'O be gone, vision fair' – where there is no orchestra, only the organ – always thrilled me.

When it came to learning a part in an opera, my usual strategy was to say to the repetiteur: "Let's go through the opera and I'll do my best to keep up."

I wouldn't keep up very well – because I couldn't sight read the music – but I would listen well. Then I would say: "Now leave me to work on this by myself. See you next week."

By then, I would know all the entries, notes and so on because I would have done the hard work bashing out the notes on my piano at home.

In my early life, on Cwrt Farm, I had access to an old 'horn' type gramophone and one record – of Frank Titterton. Later, in the very early days of my singing career, I got a gramophone from Ted Basted and I bought many records of singers but I couldn't learn arias by listening to others singing them. It is possible to pick up how a song or an aria goes from listening to recordings of it. However, all you learn is how somebody else sings it – with all their imperfections and interpretation. To learn a piece of music correctly, as it is written, you have to work at it with a repetiteur.

However, I had one record of Gigli singing the dream song from Manon – and, when I came to learn that part, I thought that I would end the aria as Gigli did on the record that I had of him.

The time came to rehearse the scene. The American soprano, Virginia McWalters - as Manon – was the only other person on the stage with me. I finished the 'dream' as Gigli did and there was a shout from Percy Hemming – the first artistic director at Covent Garden after the War.

"Don't do a 'Gigli' on us!" he bellowed.

So I couldn't copy one of my idols in performance, even though I wanted to.

It was Peter Gellhorn who taught me the part of Hermann in The Queen of Spades. It was a part that helped to make my name at Covent Garden.

When the Royal Opera company heard that Erich Kleiber was coming to Covent Garden as its musical director, we were on tour in Liverpool. David Webster, the Royal Opera's administrator, called us together – chorus and principals – to tell us the news. He said: "We have a new musical director coming to replace Karl Rankl. His name is Dr Erich Kleiber. He will be starting with us for the new season."

Some of the company knew of him. They said: "Oh no, not him!"

Erich Kleiber came to us from being the musical director of the State Opera in Berlin, where he had acquired the reputation of being something of a 'martinet'.

The first operas that Erich Kleiber was going to conduct at Covent Garden were The Magic Flute, Der Rosenkavalier and – unusually for Covent Garden – Tchaikovsky's The Queen of Spades.

After our tour of Liverpool came the summer holidays. We returned to Covent Garden in September to begin work on the new season –

and to meet Dr Kleiber. The operas had already been cast and a French tenor, called Raoul Jobin, was to sing the part of Hermann in The Queen of Spades.

Not long after we had returned to work, Sir Steuart Wilson, the deputy administrator, called me in to his office. He said: "Edgar, we're in a bit of a shambles because the French tenor has refused to come. So we want you to do the part of Hermann."

I replied: "That's a tall order. It's only three weeks until it's on!"

"I know," said Sir Steuart. "We're going to meet the conductor tomorrow [Sunday] at the Garrick Club to discuss it."

The next day – Sunday – I went to the Garrick Club. David Webster, Erich Kleiber and his wife, Eric Mitchell (the repetiteur) and his wife, Constance Shacklock, were there – among others.

The meal did not go well for me. The soup was served and, since I like some pepper in my soup, I tried to put some in my soup. Unfortunately, the top came off

● *Making up as Hermann in The Queen of Spades.*

the pepper pot and a small mount of pepper ended up making an island in the middle of my soup.

So I was not feeling at my most confident when I was introduced to Dr Kleiber. He was very softly spoken and he said to me, almost in a whisper: "You're going to be Hermann."

"Oh," I said.

"I'll see you at 10.30 tomorrow morning," he added.

The lunch ended and I came home. When I got home, I said to my wife, Nan: "I don't know how I'm going to do it!"

On the Monday, Eric Mitchell came with me to 'Room A' at the Opera House, to meet Erich Kleiber.

Dr Kleiber went through the first act of the opera with me and then sent Eric and me away with instructions to return at 5pm, when he would hear how much I had learnt of the part.

Eric did his very best with me to teach me the part. Meanwhile, I was becoming increasingly alarmed because Dr Kleiber wanted to hear me sing the whole part of Hermann after working on it for just one morning and an afternoon.

Nonetheless, we retuned to see him at 5pm.

I started to sing. After a couple of bars, Kleiber stopped me and said: "It's not like that at all."

"Well, that's what we've been doing," I said. "What am I doing wrong?"

We tried once more. Again, it was not to Kleiber's satisfaction. He stopped us and said: "Mr Evans, you've got to be a superman to do this in three weeks."

"I don't think I want to do it," I said. "Hermann's never off the stage during the opera. It's a huge part!"

"You have to be a superman," Kleiber repeated. "I'll see you tomorrow morning – at 10.30."

That evening, I telephoned Peter Gellhorn. His wife answered the phone and said that he was out and wouldn't be back until after midnight because he was conducting a performance of Der Rosenkavalier at Covent Garden.

"Well, please ask him to phone me when he comes in – whatever the time," I said.

Fortunately, Peter arrived home unexpectedly early that night – and phoned me about 11.30pm.

"Peter, I'm in a mess – but I'm not completely in a mess because I haven't said 'yes'," I explained. "Dr Kleiber wants me to sing Hermann in The Queen of Spades but I don't know whether I will be able to learn it in time. There are only three weeks until the first performance."

"Tell him you'll do it," said Peter.

"What?" I asked.

"I know all about it – the French tenor pulling out; everything," Peter continued. "Tell Kleiber that you can sing the part if you have me to teach it to you. Everything will be alright."

So, at 10.30 the next morning, I went to see Dr Kleiber. In the room with him were a number of repetiteurs – except Peter Gellhorn. They were all discussing the finer points of the music in the opera, since they were working with different singers on their parts in the opera.

Dr Kleiber asked me: "Well, are you going to do it?"

"Yes – if I can work on the part with Peter Gellhorn."

It was embarrassing for me to say this in front of all the other repetiteurs.

"Who is Peter Gellhorn?"

"He's the one who conducted Rosenkavalier here at the Opera House last night."

"Very well then – but see me again, at 11.30 tomorrow morning," Kleiber said.

I found Peter Gellhorn and we began work on the opera about 11am that day. We finished about 10pm. By then, I had almost gone through the entire opera without me having to play any of it on the piano.

By the time we finished for the night I had become used to Peter's way of teaching and it appealed to me – or, at least, it was memorable for me. For example, Peter suggested that I thought in 'tonic sol-fa' when I had to cope with singing awkward intervals.

We began work the next day at 10am and, by 11.30 when I was due to see Dr Kleiber, I had memorised the first section of my part.

"Go and see Dr Kleiber now," said Peter. "You're safe in the part. What I have taught you is in the score. Kleiber can't quibble with any of that."

I set off to see Dr Kleiber and, as I approached the room where he was rehearsing the other principals, aided by a piano, I heard one of my cues coming up. I opened the door and – right on cue – sang.

"Mein Gott!" muttered Kleiber, "he knows it!"

He turned to me and said: "You're not to worry anymore. You have come in at the right time. It doesn't matter how many mistakes you make now – we can put it right."

I went back to Peter briefly, to 'clean' my part up and then worked with the 'ordinary' repetiteurs to become thoroughly familiar with the part.

Rehearsals moved to the stage at the Opera House and it was – mostly – plain sailing from there on.

However, The Daily Herald, (14th December 1950), reported: 'Edgar Evans, the Welsh tenor ... is to sing one of opera's most difficult roles, Hermann the gambler in Tchaikovsky's Queen of Spades (Covent Garden, 21st December)...At rehearsal yesterday he ended a drinking song by hurling away the goblet in fine style; it knocked out one of the chorus.'

During one of the rehearsals, Dr Kleiber – knowing that English was not my first language - asked me: "What is 'very good' in Welsh?"

"Da iawn," I replied.

So Dr Kleiber continued to say this to me while I was singing. All went well with the first performance. Dr Kleiber gave everyone every cue. He was very easy to work with. I thoroughly enjoyed the experience.

In the book 'Erich Kleiber, a Memoir by John Russell (published by Andre Deutsch, 1957), Russell recounts: 'As Hermann, the doomed gambler, Mr Edgar Evans had a particular success: 'It was astonishing,' The Times said, 'what its frank theatricality did to loosen our Mr Edgar Evans' dramatic abilities, which hitherto have been more latent than realised, however good

● *With Edith Coates (the Countess) in The Queen of Spades.*

his singing – which was indeed energised by this new-found freedom.' Mr Evans had hesitated, in point of fact, to undertake this taxing part, and the story of how Kleiber coaxed him into doing it is still often told at Covent Garden. 'It doesn't matter how many mistakes you make,' he would say. 'I don't mind. I like it. It's what I'm there for. I'll always get you out if it, so just go ahead and do as you like.'

According to Montague Haltrecht's biography of David Webster (1975): 'The Queen of Spades brought forward many house singers. Raoul Jobin had been invited to sing Hermann but suddenly Edgar

Evans received an invitation to lunch with Webster and arrived to find Kleiber there too, as well as Steuart Wilson and Constance Shacklock. There was a possibility that he might do Hermann instead. He shook pepper nervously into his soup, the pepper-top and a deal of pepper fell in, but he made no comment and drank it just the same, and with burning mouth agreed to take on the part (Of course, this latter part of the sentence is not absolutely correct). The read-through was next morning at ten o'clock, and that evening at five o'clock he was asked to sing. The first bars were wrong. After five or six bars he wanted to give up.

"'How can I do it?"

"'Ah,' said Kleiber warningly, "you have to be a superman."

'Kleiber was a tyrant if he didn't get what he wanted. There were only three weeks of rehearsal before going on stage, and the first night was four weeks away. Evans was given till next morning to decide. He rang Peter Gellhorn who agreed to teach him the role, and also advised him to tell Kleiber he'd need a few days alone. In fact Gellhorn taught him the role in a single day, going over it from ten in the morning until ten at night. The following day at eleven Edgar Evans went to Kleiber and they began on the second act.

"'Mein Gott!" Kleiber exclaimed. "He knows it."

A benevolent expression usurped his mask of amazement.

"'Now you can be easy. I shall not worry you.'"

Afterwards, Dr Kleiber said to me: "I have put you on a pedestal. You must not do any more little parts. You do the main parts from now on."

Since Dr Kleiber was the musical director at Covent Garden, it was extremely fortunate for me that he took that view. For example, I had already sung the small part of Andres in Wozzeck but, after the advent of Dr Kleiber and my portrayal of Hermann in The Queen of Spades, I always sang the much larger part of the Drum Major in Alban Berg's opera.

Moreover, a little while later – in 1952 – Erich Kleiber took me to Rome Opera to sing (in German) the part of Froh in Das Rheingold that he was conducting there. Three principals from Covent Garden were invited to go to sing in Rome: Otakar Kraus, the Czech baritone, who had previously sung at La Scala, Milan, in 1951, Frederick

Dalberg, the South African bass who had previously sung with the Berlin State Opera, and me. Indeed, the Liverpool Daily Post (7th March 1953) speculated that I would be 'probably the first Welshman to sing at the Rome Opera House'.

● *Edgar as Hermann in The Queen of Spades.*

Chapter twenty one

Miscellany

A date with Callas

Montague Haltrecht, in, 'The Quiet Showman', the biography of David Webster (published by Collins, 1975), writes: 'The 50th anniversary of Verdi's death, in January 1951, had come and gone without any celebration at Covent Garden. Webster felt guilty. The Sicilian Vespers had been discussed, possibly to be given in preference even to 'Wozzeck' as Kleiber's second new production at the house. Webster...liked the idea of a new Verdi opera, if only because it would help him strengthen the Italian repertory, which from the start had given far more trouble than the German... At Covent Garden the work was going to be given in English, with Edgar Evans, probably, beside one or two outstanding artists from Kleiber's Florence production. Boris Christoff had been in it, he wanted to work with Kleiber again, and he spoke English. The soprano too spoke English, and although she was new it seemed that they couldn't do better: she'd caused quite a stir in this Vespers under Kleiber. She was Greek, and had subsequently made a successful La Scala debut. Like Christoff, she was also going to be asked to sing in English. Now, what was her name? Webster wasn't good on names. Oh yes. It was – Maria Callas.

'These plans for a Covent Garden 'Sicilian Vespers' came to nothing.'

Dressers

For many years, during my time at the Opera House, the dresser who looked after the male artists was Leon. It was he who spotted, one evening, that I had injured the back of my hand during a scene in Carmen involving a sabre fight with Rhydderch Davies, who was playing the part of Zuniga *(see 'Injuries' below)*.

However, in my very early years at Covent Garden there was a dresser named Horace. He had been a dresser at Covent Garden since before the War.

One day, he said to me: "I had a gold sovereign (tip) from Caruso once."

Apparently, that evening, Caruso had been 'taken short' before going on stage to sing. It was too late to do anything except for Caruso to relieve himself against the scenery just off stage. Unfortunately, the water seeped through to the dressing rooms below – and some of it fell on Horace's head.

After the performance, Horace mentioned to the Opera House management that there appeared to have been a leak and that he had got wet. Overhearing him, Caruso owned up – and gave Horace a sovereign (a lot of money in those days) for his trouble.

Erich Kleiber

Dr Erich Kleiber, the conductor who, perhaps, did more than any other to transform Edgar Evans from a 'house tenor' into a 'star' performer, died in Zurich after a heart attack in 1956. He was 65.

Erich Kleiber twice resigned from the Berlin State Opera because of political interference. In 1935, after 12 years as director of the Opera, he resigned in protest against Nazi interference and left Germany. Then, in March 1955, shortly before the opera moved back into its restored building on the Unter Den Linden, he told the Communist controller that he must resign again because: "The spirit of the old State Opera cannot reign in the new house."

Most of the years from 1936 to 1949 he spent in Buenos Aires, where he was conductor in chief of the German opera season at the Teatro Colon. He also toured extensively in North and South America as well as Europe. He was guest conductor at Covent Garden between November 1950 and February 1951 and in 1952. He took over the direction of the London Philharmonic Orchestra for a while in 1948 and conducted the orchestra again the following year.

Gentleman and player

On Friday 11th July 1952, I sang at a concert given by The Hallé Orchestra, conducted by Sir John Barbirolli, at the Royal Hall in Harrogate. Afterwards, Sir John, who was a great fan of cricket, said to me: "Edgar, will you come and have dinner with me tonight at the cricket club in Harrogate?"

I was not a sportsman and I have never taken much interest in sport but the thought of a dinner was attractive and so I agreed.

That evening, I found myself being introduced, by Sir John, to Len – later Sir Len – Hutton, one of the greatest batsmen that Yorkshire has produced and, at that time, the holder of the world record for the highest individual score in Test cricket (364 v Australia, made at The Oval in 1938). It was a very pleasant evening and Len was excellent company – even if he understood as much about opera singing as I did about making runs in a Test Match!

Hetty the Hen

According to a report in the Star (3rd November 1959): 'Hetty the Hen interrupted a full dress rehearsal of the Russian opera Boris Godunov at the Royal Opera House, Covent Garden, today.

Hetty, one of several hens carried on stage in a wicker basket in the second act, pecked her way to freedom and with much clucking and fluttering of wings began sprinting about the stage.

Tenor Edgar Evans, son of a Welsh farmer, demonstrated his knowledge of rural arts by diving in a tackle on Hetty. He was applauded by the private audience and the opera went on.'

When it came to the performance, Leslie Ayre, the reviewer from The Evening News, wrote: 'Edgar Evans sang the Pretender much better than his immediate predecessor in the role but his big scene with Marina (Constance Shacklock) lacked final charm. And again, the Inn Scene – though robust and assisted by hens which clucked as though following the conductor's baton – did not flare up into full boisterousness.'

The Stage, while complementing Edith Coates on her performance as the Hostess, concluded: 'Perhaps the real hens in this scene were not a good idea – their amusing obbligato brought us dangerously near to Clara Cluck.'

Injuries

One evening – in July 1958 - I was singing Don Jose in Carmen at the Opera House. On this particular occasion, there was only one man – not the usual two – to hold me back during the fight scene with Escamillo. While the scene was developing, I asked the man – whose name was Hamish Macmillan – why there weren't two men to hold me back tonight.

Hamish said: "Oh, the other man's ill. I can do it by myself."

When the time came, Hamish put his arms around my waist and pulled so hard that he broke my ribs. It was so painful that I could not give full voice to the angry outburst that I was supposed to sing then. However, I did finish the performance – albeit in great pain.

Reporting this incident, the Evening News revealed a possible reason for Hamish's roughness: 'It was the third act of Carmen. The

● *About to get some broken ribs in Carmen.*

floorboards of Covent Garden creaked as 14-stone tenor Edgar Evans (he's Don Jose) collided with 15-stone Hamish Macmillan (he's a smuggler).

Result? Evans, a Welshman, cracked a rib. Macmillan, a Scot, apologised. And tenor James Johnston, an Irishman, will deputise tonight.

Five years ago, the order was reversed. In a sword-swinging scene Evans landed Macmillan, ex-goalkeeping understudy to Frank Swift [Manchester City], in hospital with a cut vein…'

After the performance I went to the Charing Cross Hospital and they bandaged me up so that I could hardly breathe. So, when I got home, Nan and Huw ripped off the bandages. That was equally as painful since it pulled off a lot of hair too!

Incidentally, broken ribs were not the only injury I sustained while singing the role of Don Jose in Carmen. One evening – in July 1954 – I received, by an accident of misjudgement, a two inch gash in the back of my hand during a scene involving a sabre fight with Rhydderch Davies, who was playing the part of Zuniga (see 'Dressers' above).

Initially, no one – not even I – seemed to know where the blood was coming from. Allegedly, seeing my predicament, one of the chorus tore a rough bandage from his shirt and this bandage was passed from hand to hand among the chorus in an effort to reach me – but no one seemed to be able to get close enough to give it to me.

It was only when I got back to my dressing room that Leon, the dresser, spotted that I was bleeding. So, the cut was bandaged and I completed the performance without further mishap. I had hoped that the audience hadn't really noticed what had happened but, the next day, the incident was reported in the newspapers – including the Daily Herald, Daily Sketch, News Chronicle, Daily Worker, Daily Mail, Manchester Guardian and The Times. The incident was even reported in the Cape Argus in South Africa!

However, the Manchester Guardian found a sting in the tail of this incident. It reminded its readers: 'Edgar Evans, the tenor whose hand was cut in last week's Covent Garden Carmen, was able to finish the two remaining acts of the opera. This is an occupational risk with the new realism in opera production. In the old days the tenor and baritone crossed swords very gingerly indeed; and even when they did stab one another they sang instead of bleeding, as an American wag once noted ruefully. Mr Evans' mishap, however, though it was perhaps the most dramatic thing that happened on stage, at least earned him the consolation of notice in the news pages while sparing his dignity, unlike that of the rival Don Jose at Sadler's Wells whose split breeches in January last caused the curtain to be rung down and special editions to be issued.' (Manchester Guardian, 12th July 1954)

Keeping abreast of the situation

The outstanding American mezzo-soprano, Marilyn Horne, had made her operatic debut, at the age of 20, in the role of Hata in Smetana's The Bartered Bride for the Los Angeles Guild Opera in the autumn of 1954. But she had her first great success in Germany in 1960 as Marie in Wozzeck – a role she later performed to great acclaim in San Francisco - and she made her Covent Garden debut in October 1964 in this role too.

At the dress rehearsal for this production – at which, traditionally, the Friends of Covent Garden are allowed to watch – Marilyn and I were working through a scene where the Drum Major is making advances to Marie.

I was going through the traditional stage business – of caressing her arms and body – and had put my arms around her waist, when Marilyn suddenly grabbed my hands and brought them up to her breasts.

I was startled but she whispered to me, as the scene continued: "Here. Play with these!"

Seeing the move, the audience in the packed Opera House – shocked by my apparent daring - gasped audibly.

King of the Garden

Once, while rehearsing the role of the king in Masked Ball at Covent Garden, the time came for me to make my first entrance onto the stage.

I entered – only to be told by the producer, Günther Rennert, that I hadn't walked like a king and needed to learn how to do it properly.

Günther, at the time one of the world's leading opera producers, then demonstrated for me how he thought a king should walk.

When he had finished his demonstration, the stage manager, Andy Anderson, said to me – for everyone to hear: "Well, you walk more like a king than he does!"

Günther roared with laughter and he and I became firm friends from that moment on. Later, we even went to the Motor Show at Earl's Court together!

● *With Helena Verte in A Masked Ball.*

Overseas

Writing about Erich Kleiber, in the biography of David Webster, 'The Quiet Showman' by Montague Haltrecht (1975), Haltrecht writes: 'Kleiber arranged for singers to study abroad and he promised foreign appearances. (Constance) Shacklock was the first. She sang in Amsterdam and The Hague during the Wagner Festival in November 1951...In Kleiber's 1952 Rome 'Ring', (Sylvia) Fisher was the Sieglinde and Otakar Kraus Alberich, with Edgar Evans and Frederick Dalberg also in the cast.'

Producers

Not every producer is easy to work with. Once, we were rehearsing La Traviata at the London Welsh Hall in the Gray's Inn Road (because of lack of space at the Opera House) and the producer was Tyrone Guthrie.

What a character he was! He was nothing if not forthright about everything – to an extent that was often embarrassing.

In one scene, Jess Walters – one of the nicest and mildest mannered men you could meet – was singing a duet with Audrey Bowman. Guthrie listened intently to the whole duet, which had been sung with great sensitivity and was very moving. At the end, he shouted: "Jess, I never heard a f***ing word you sang!"

Pronunciation

One night, in Aida, Marian Nowakowski – playing the king – greeted Radames not with the traditional words, 'Naught can be denied thee on such a day' but with, 'Naught can be denied thee on Saturday'. Although unnoticed by the audience, it caused some amusement on stage.

This story was told to me – and others - by Norman Walker who, like Nowakowski, was a bass. So there may have been an element of professional jealousy or envy in this story. As the saying is in Welsh: 'cythrel y canu' – the 'devilment in singing'.

Politics

Music is music. You don't mix music with politics. There was no 'backlash' to performing Richard Strauss or Wagner's music at Covent Garden straight after the War – even though Strauss had collaborated with the Nazis and Wagner's music had come to be strongly identified with the Third Reich.

The conductor, Erich Kleiber was not a Jew but he disagreed with Hitler and the Nazi policies so much that he left Germany to work at the Colon Opera House in Argentina with the State Opera there.

Once, we were rehearsing Richard Strauss' Salome at Covent Garden with an American baritone singing the part of John the Baptist. At one part in the opera – where John the Baptist is singing from under the stage – Karl Rankl called the American baritone up on stage to take him to task over some small mistake. As he did, the baritone muttered to me: "That's one that Hitler missed!"

Recollections - I

According to Brian Godfrey – a member of the chorus at the Hoffnung Interplanetary Music Festivals in which Edgar Evans sang, in 1958 and 1959 (see appendix two) – "Edgar Evans arrived on stage at the Royal Festival Hall during one of the Hoffnung Interplanetary Music Festivals. On seeing the conductor - Norman del Mar - he sang, to the notes of the aria 'Cielo e mar' from Ponchielli's opera La Gioconda: 'Cielo! del Mar'.

"Sadly, some of the in-jokes were lost, I think, on much of the audience who were basically a concert rather than an opera audience."

Recollections - I1

According to Peter Jenkin, a well known repetiteur in Hertfordshire for many years, his singing teacher – Arthur Fear (born in 1902), who had had a career as a baritone, singing roles with the Carl Rosa and Sadler's Wells companies – had once complained of having a 'frog' in his throat and feared that he would be unable to sing. On the eve of the concert he was to give, Arthur Fear had telephoned Edgar Evans for advice. In reply, Edgar Evans allegedly said: "Oh! Put a 'Tyrosette' [a throat lozenge] under your tongue when you go to bed and you'll be alright! They're very good for 'frogs'!"

Recollections - I1

Martin Hill, of Wolverhampton, wrote: 'I saw Edgar Evans on stage at Birmingham in the 1950s in a performance of Carmen in which he took the part of Don Jose – with Constance Shacklock singing Carmen.

'From what I can remember, some 50 years later, Edgar Evans had a strong and sweet tenor voice and was very dramatic on stage.'

Recollections - IV

'I must have seen and heard Edgar Evans in everything he sang at Covent Garden,' wrote Hilary Tangye, of Barnes in south west London. 'The role in which I best remember him is Hermann in Queen of Spades – particularly in the barrack room scene, which was spine chilling. I have seen a number of other Hermanns over the years and only one ever managed to excel him.

'Of course, the old production was wonderful, and was conducted by Erich Kleiber. To my mind, Kleiber always managed to make singers give of their best.

'Evans sang such a great variety of roles from Don Jose, Dmitri in Boris Godunov to roles in Wozzeck and Salome. I look back on those years with great pleasure.'

Recollections - V

One of Edgar Evans' singing pupils, Len Williams – who runs

'Opera Sempre' in Huddersfield, in Yorkshire – recalled: 'Before I had lessons with Edgar, I studied with Redvers Llewellyn, the famous bel canto Verdi baritone. Redvers had been a soloist at Sadler's Wells when Edgar was in the chorus and, as a senior but fellow Welshman, Redvers looked after Edgar there and made him feel welcome.

'One day, I asked Redvers what Edgar's voice was like. Redvers was always highly critical of other singers but he said: "He had a full blooded tenor voice." That was praise indeed.

When Redvers died, I went to Delme Bryn Jones, who was very helpful. Later, he took me to Edgar and I studied with him for four years or so. Edgar taught on the same bel canto lines as Redvers and Delme. The fact that Edgar had sung a great many roles was a great help.

'I think that they worked him so hard at Covent Garden that he nearly lost his health. When he went to record with Vic Oliver he was not feeling well. But, as he said: "I brought it off!" He certainly did! Bless him.'

Technology and television

In his autobiography, 'Mr Showbusiness, the autobiography of Vic Oliver' (published by George G Harrap & Co Ltd, 1954), Vic Oliver described 'This Is Show Business', a television programme – broadcast live, on the BBC, in 1951 – which aimed to present the very best performers in every branch of contemporary show business in the UK. Representing 'drama' were Trevor Howard and Margaret Johnson. 'Comedy' came from Arthur Askey and Terry-Thomas; with Bernard Braden and Barbara Kelly representing 'radio'; Coco the Clown representing 'the circus'; Berisova and Domini Callaghan representing the 'ballet'; Jack and Daphne Barker representing 'cabaret' and Harvey Alan, Amy Shuard and me representing 'opera'.

We performed Il Trovatore, with me singing the role of Manrico and Peter Glossop as Luna. Because of the size of the studios, the orchestra was in the BBC studios at Delaware Road – a long way away from the BBC Television Centre where the singers were. In what was considered a great triumph of technology, the BBC arranged a series of monitors to allow the singers to see the conductor and hear the orchestra as it played the music, thus defeating the time-lag caused by the vast distances between singers and orchestra.

I appeared on this annual programme again – on 31st May 1954. This time, the cast included character actor Eric Barker, representing television, Frances Day representing cabaret; Brian Reece (drama); Freddie Sales (music hall); juggler Pierre Bel (the circus); Dennis Brain, playing part of a Horn Concerto ('the concert platform'), and myself – representing opera – singing 'Nessun Dorma' from Turandot.

John Howells remembers: "seeing Edgar Evans on my parents' television in about 1953 or so. He was all 'dolled up' in what, I suppose, was Chinese costume performing 'Nessun Dorma'.

"Those early televised – live - operatic performances must have been an ordeal. I once saw Lawrence Payne, who was better known as an actor, come 'unstuck' during the final bars of 'Celeste Aida'. An attempt to exonerate him was then made by the comedian/conductor, Vic Oliver, who explained that Mr Payne had just flown back from entertaining the troops in BAOR and was tired."

Temper tantrums

Rehearsing for one production of Boris Godunov at Covent Garden – not the production that involved 'the horse' (see Chapter 13) – Boris Christoff threw a temper tantrum and made it impossible for the opera to be rehearsed on the set.

So Constance Shacklock and I had to rehearse our duet on stage in front of the 'iron (safety) curtain'. This meant that we had between 18 inches and two feet in which to move – and, of course, sing.

Unfortunately, the top had also been taken off the prompt box and, concentrating on singing and acting the duet, I failed to see the open prompt box and promptly fell into it, landing awkwardly on my knee. I screamed. It was very painful indeed and I thought I had broken my leg.

In the end, that evening – for the performance of Salome – I sang the part of Narraboth, the captain of the royal guard, while being heavily bandaged and moving very gingerly indeed. My characterisation that evening must have puzzled even the most knowledgeable of the cognoscenti.

● *Edgar, in his early days as a professional singer...*

● *in his early days as a professor at the Royal College of Music...*

● *signing autographs...*

● *and saying farewell to Nan and Huw when off to sing in Toulouse.*

Appendix one: Press notices

Organised by the Post Warden and Wardens of Post 22 at the Lord Melchett Hall, Compayne Gardens, Hampstead, last Saturday, a concert in aid of the RAF Benevolent Fund proved both a financial and musical success...Edgar Evans, who gave two selections of songs, had a good voice but not a great variety of tone...

Jay Wilbur, of 'Hi-Gang' fame, was there in person and auctioned three photos of Bebe Daniels and Ben Lyon. A basket of apples was also auctioned. Altogether the RAF Benevolent Fund benefited to the amount of £40. (Hampstead Gazette, 1940)

◆◆◆◆◆◆

Mr Eugene Iskoldoff quaintly comperes his own Anglo-Russian Merry Go Round, a novel mixture of revue, music and ballet, rich in colours and abounding in animal spirits...Mr Edgar Evans, a Welsh tenor discovered by Mr Iskoldoff has a vivid military scene, 'La Reve passe', which includes a novel background effect. The large range of costumes is brilliant and artistic. (West Lancashire Evening Gazette 24th October 1944)

◆◆◆◆◆◆

... Anglo-Russian Merry Go Round has many excellent features, not least the really fine standard of singing of the whole company and of such solo artists as Zoya Valevska and Edgar Evans. (Manchester Evening News, 26th September 1944)

◆◆◆◆◆◆

The Ceramic City Choir closed their season with the annual Easter performance of Handel's Messiah in the Victoria Hall, Hanley, last night, when Dr Malcolm Sargent conducted the work before an audience which crowded all parts of the hall to the doors... Mr Edgar Evans, the tenor, was a newcomer, and no doubt some hesitance – at the beginning of 'Thy rebuke' for instance – could be set down to nervousness. He has a fine voice, rich in quality and ample in resonance but inclined to throatiness now and again. His best singing was in 'Thou shalt break them'. (Evening Sentinel, 26th April 1946)

◆◆◆◆◆◆

The Gay Revue, Bernard Delfont's new vaudeville entertainment at the Commodore Theatre, Ryde, opened on Friday week... Mr Edgar Evans, a tenor of fine tone and excellent range, contributes largely to the success of the entertainment... (Isle of Wight Times, 13th June 1946)

◆◆◆◆◆◆

Two members of the cast [of the Travelling Opera Group] – Nina Barbone and Edgar Evans – are shortly joining the Covent Garden Opera Company... No better tenor than Edgar Evans has ever been heard in Tavistock, for his voice was one of exquisite beauty. (The Cornish Times. 15th November 1946)

◆◆◆◆◆◆

Letter to Edgar Evans from Hubert Foss, editor of 'Music Lover', 28th March 1947:

I was never a flatterer but... I should like to congratulate you on the splendid performance you put up on Tuesday night in Manon. My heartiest congratulations... I think you have possibilities that you have not yet discovered...you might possibly become a more experienced actor than the others...

◆◆◆◆◆◆

There were good performances... at Covent Garden, where a promising young British tenor, Edgar Evans, had his first big chance as the hero of Manon and took it. Result, an enthusiastic solo curtain for him. (News of the World, 30th March 1947)

✦✦✦✦✦✦

I have not heard Edgar Evans before, but I shall hope to do so often. He is an admirable des Grieux with a fine voice, but he must lose that habit of watching the conductor. (Catholic Herald, 3rd April 1947)

✦✦✦✦✦✦

In the Covent Garden production of Manon last night, the part of the Chevalier des Grieux was taken by a newcomer, Edgar Evans. His voice, if of no great power, has a very pleasant timbre and is produced with ease – qualities which are especially important in Manon.

But the most notable thing about his performance was the fact that it realised perfectly the elegant as well as the sentimental character of the melodic line. High notes were not treated as occasions for exhibiting the power of the singer's lungs and we heard the music as Massenet meant it to be sung. (The Daily Telegraph, 18th April 1947)

✦✦✦✦✦✦

Mr Evans...proved immensely popular and used his powerful voice with admirable effect... (Somerset County Herald, 6th December 1947)

✦✦✦✦✦✦

Deputising for Mr Midgley (in a performance of Strauss' Der Rosenkavalier given by the Covent Garden Opera Company in Birmingham) as the Italian tenor, Edgar Evans sings so fervently that one is surprised the Marschallin did not forget Octavian, Ochs and the general mêlée and give him, at the very least, the job he was after. (Birmingham Post, 1948)

✦✦✦✦✦✦

(In Boris Godunov)...there is fine work from Constance Shacklock, Howell Glynne, Richard Lewis and Edgar Evans. The latter is the most satisfactory tenor I've heard at Covent Garden since the Vienna were there. He sings well even on the tired-looking white horse which (the producer, Peter) Brook mistakenly introduces into the last scene. (What's On, 21st May 1948)

✦✦✦✦✦✦

... Edgar Evans' Froh was remarkable. Much may be expected of this talented young tenor. (The Daily Telegraph, 13th May 1949)

✦✦✦✦✦✦

Edgar Evans (as Hermann in The Queen of Spades) sang with great emotional power and versatility as the young officer going mad in his quest for a secret of gambling success. (The Daily Herald, 22nd December 1950)

✦✦✦✦✦✦

Edgar Evans as Hermann proved that he is now an actor as well as a very agreeable tenor. (The Observer, 24th December 1950)

✦✦✦✦✦✦

The first night of Vaughan Williams' Pilgrim's Progress, on Thursday 26th April at Covent Garden, was an occasion long to be remembered by those privileged to attend it...Edgar Evans, as the Interpreter and later as the Heavenly Messenger, took the stage by singing and deportment better than that of the rest of the company. (Musical Times, June 1951)

✦✦✦✦✦✦

Edgar Evans (Calaf, in Turandot) revealed a power, richness and control which, on last night's showing, place him in the forefront of contemporary British tenors. (The Daily Telegraph, 12th January 1952)

✦✦✦✦✦✦

Edgar Evans gave a magnificent performance as Captain Vere (Billy Budd). His acting was as distinguished as his singing... (South Wales Evening Post, 8th March 1952)

✦✦✦✦✦✦

...Edgar Evans...sings Puccini delightfully in the Wagnerian tradition... (News Chronicle, 2nd March 1952)

✦✦✦✦✦✦

As Captain Vere (Billy Budd), Edgar Evans showed great skill in portraying the conflicting emotions of the part and, vocally, he was excellent. (Glasgow Herald, 29th March 1952)

✦✦✦✦✦✦

The part of Captain Vere, originally taken by Peter Pears, found in Edgar Evans an artist of the most distinguished quality. (The

Scotsman, 31st March 1951)

✦✦✦✦✦✦

The change was in the part of Captain Vere, which was taken over by Mr Edgar Evans... Mr Evans has not Mr Pears' authoritative bearing but his voice is a little harder in grain and in the main opera is to that extent an improvement in conveying the man of action on deck; in prologue and epilogue Mr Pears is more successful in suggesting the reflective observer of life. (The Times, 28th April 1952)

✦✦✦✦✦✦

Musically the production (A Masked Ball) is a landmark in the career of the tenor Edgar Evans. He cuts a gallant figure as the lighthearted king and his vocal resources have developed to the Covent Garden scale. While it still remains for him to purify his resonance, he scored a distinguished success. (The Daily Telegraph, 24th October 1952)

✦✦✦✦✦✦

Joan Sutherland sang Amelia and Edgar Evans the King (in A Masked Ball) both in full pleasant voice – much too good to admit complaint about their acting. (Manchester Daily Mail, 31st March 1953)

✦✦✦✦✦✦

Peter Grimes opened the new season at the Royal Opera House on 20th April...Edgar Evans appeared as Grimes and gave a thoughtful account of the role. There was, however, a suggestion of anxiety if not, indeed, of strain in his performance which added yet another complex to a character already overburdened with them. (Musical Opinion, May 1954)

✦✦✦✦✦✦

The change of cast in The Tales of Hoffmann at Covent Garden last night brought forward several new principals. Edgar Evans was well suited to the role of Hoffmann and sang with great conviction and assurance... (The Daily Telegraph, 24th November 1954)

[I took over the role of Hoffmann from Julius Patzak. He was the first Hoffmann at Covent Garden after the War and was not only a fine tenor but was also noted for his interpretation of this role. It was a great honour to take over the role from him.]

✦✦✦✦✦✦

Edgar Evans, singing (the role of Don Jose in Carmen) for the first time after his long illness, started tentatively and it was not until the Flower Song was past that he relaxed and the voice flowed evenly. Then he produced some strong and dramatic singing, and the last act derived much of its impact – and it was a very considerable impact – from his spirited attack and confident touch. (South Wales Argus, 24th February 1956)

✦✦✦✦✦✦

Of the other soloists, I would pick out Edgar Evans as the Drum Major (in Wozzeck). He gave a fine performance of the swaggering officer and bully who expected his own way in everything, pleasing to the women and not above beating his own men. It is nice to hear Mr Edgar Evans, who is an old hand at The Opera House, sing this part as if it were written for him. He is suited to this style and deserves the success he made of it. (The New Daily, 7th December 1960)

✦✦✦✦✦✦

...there are first-rate sketches of the local dignitaries (in the Visit of the Old Lady by von Einem) by Alan Crowfoot, Derek Hammond-Stroud and Don Garrard, and of the mysterious butler by Edgar Evans. (The Sunday Times, 3rd June 1973)

● *Edgar, with Elsie Morrison, in Arwel Hughes' opera, Menna.*

Appendix two: Workload

This list of Edgar Evans' performances may be extensive but it is by no means exclusive. The list has been compiled from the many programmes that Edgar Evans accumulated over the years.

It illustrates the diversity in Edgar Evans' career – in terms of, for example the:

Types of venue – from concert halls around the country to the Royal Albert Hall.

Types and styles of performance - from the ornate masque of 'The Fairy Queen', via 'the Messiah' to the informality of a St David's Day

● *Edgar (seated, centre) as Captain Davidson in Richard Rodney Bennett's Victory.*

dinner and concert in Southampton.

Other artists appearing - from Kenneth Horne, Richard Murdoch and Benny Hill to Constant Lambert and Sir John Barbirolli.

Music performed – from 17th century songs by William and Henry Lawes to contemporary Welsh ballads and, in operatic terms, from Henry Purcell's The Fairy Queen to Richard Rodney Bennett's Victory via Don Jose in Bizet's Carmen.

Programmes:

Falstaff (Wednesday 20th April & Saturday 23rd April 1938) at Sadler's Wells
Edgar Evans appeared in the Chorus.
Performance conducted by Warwick Braithwaite.

Concert (22nd March 1939) broadcast on BBC Radio

Performers: The BBC Welsh Orchestra, conducted by Idris Lewis, Edgar Evans

Programme included: Hark, hark, the ecch'ing air (Purcell), Sigh no more, ladies (Aiken), There is a garden in her face (Campion, arr Keel), To Music (Schubert), I love thee (Grieg), Autumn (C Alison Crompton)

Concert (15th July 1939) broadcast on BBC Radio

Performers: The BBC Welsh Orchestra, conducted by Mansel Thomas, Edgar Evans

Programme included: Passing By (Purcell), Where'er you walk (Handel), Love's Poem (Idris Lewis), The Lavender Lass (Alan Murray), Phillis has such charming graces (Anthony Young, arr Lane Wilson), The Old House (Frederick O'Connor).

Annual Concert (Friday 27th March 1942) in Liskeard

Performers: Nancy Barber, Grace Nevern, Edgar Evans, Murray Davies, the Liskeard & District Choral Society

Programme included: On with the motley (Pagliacci), Where'er you walk (Handel), Your tiny hand is frozen (La Boheme), English Rose (Merrie England), You are my heart's delight (Lehar).

Popular Concert (Sunday 19th April 1942) at the Ritz Theatre, Stroud

Performers: Tommy Seymour, Bert Lester, the Three Wrens, the Harringtons, Herbert Aldridge, Edgar Evans, The Bourne Sisters

Programme included: You are my heart's delight (Lehar), English Rose (Merrie England), Where'er you walk (Handel), Bless this house (Brahe).

British-American Concert (Thursday 30th May 1943) at Cheltenham Town Hall

Performers: John Balestrieri, Mamie Brown, Edgar Evans, Louis Pollack.

Programme included: English Rose (Merrie England), Where'er you walk (Handel)

CEMA concert (Sunday 9th January 1944) in Wednesbury

Performers: Gladys Corlett, Edgar Evans, Lillian Niblette.

Programme included: Where'er you walk (Handel), Sigh no more, ladies (Aiken), I love thee (Grieg), To music (Schubert), The stars were shining brightly (Tosca), Largo (Xerxes).

Concert (Saturday 19th February 1944) at the Girls' School, Sidcup

Performers: Bryan Gipps, Esther Salaman, Frank Thomas, Edgar Evans.

Programme included: Where'er you walk (Handel), Sigh no more, ladies (Aiken), Phillis has such charming graces (Lane Wilson), Silent Worship (Handel), To music (Schubert), On with the motley (Pagliacci).

Concert (Sunday 20th February 1944) at the Town Hall, Leamington Spa

Performers: Jan Berenska and his orchestra, Edgar Evans.

Programme included: On with the motley (Pagliacci), I love thee (Grieg), Sigh no more, ladies (Aiken).

Elijah (Good Friday 7th April 1944) at Worthing Town Hall

Performers: Florence Austral, Margaret Balfour, Edgar Evans, Henry Gill, conducted by Francis Crute.

Concert (Sunday 17th December 1944) at the Bournemouth Pavilion

Performers: Edgar Evans, Percy Whitlock, The Municipal Orchestra

Programme included: Lend me your aid (Irene), English Rose (Merrie England), God will remember (Myers).

A Grand Evening Concert (Tuesday 9th January 1945) at Shiloh Chapel, Lampeter

Performers: Edgar Evans, Myra Jones, the Teifi Singers

Programme included: Where'er you walk (Handel), 'Largo' (Xerxes), Your tiny hand is frozen (La Boheme), Lend me your aid (Irene), Come back to Sorrento (Curtis), English Rose (Merrie England), La donna e mobile (Rigoletto), Yr Hen Gerddor / The Old Minstrel (D Pughe Evans), Panis Angelicus (Franck), On with the Motley (Pagliacci).

A Night with the Stars (Wednesday 17th October 1945) at Ebenzer Chapel, Newcastle-Emlyn

Performers: Margaret Evans, Edgar Evans, Mervyn Griffiths, Edward Morgan

Programme included: Ombra mai fu (Xerxes), Lend me your aid (Irene), On with the Motley (Pagliacci), Come back to Sorrento (Curtis).

The Messiah (Handel) (Thursday 25th April 1946) at the Victoria Hall, Hanley, Staffordshire

Performers: Ceinwen Rowlands, Kathleen Ferrier, Edgar Evans, Robert Easton, The Ceramic City Choir

Performance conducted by Dr Malcolm Sargent.

Massed Band Concert (Sunday 5th May 1946) at Exeter Theatre Royal

Performers: Edgar Evans, Muriel Rae, the massed bands of the 2nd Battalion, The Devonshire Regiment and the 1st Battalion, The Duke of Cornwall's Light Infantry

Programme included: Where'er you walk (Handel).

Concert (Sunday 26th May 1946) at the Bournemouth Pavilion

Performers: Edgar Evans, Arthur Coleman, The Municipal Orchestra

Programme included: Lend me your aid (Irene), Sigh no more, ladies (Aikin), Silent Worship (Handel).

The Ephesian Matron (performed with 'The Partisans') (Tuesday 28th to Friday 31st May 1946) at the St Pancras Town Hall

Edgar Evans played the Centurion.

Performance conducted by Geoffrey Corbett.

Celebrity Concert (Sunday 25th August 1946) at the Grand Pavilion, Llandrindod Wells

Performers: Essie Ackland, Edgar Evans, Grahame Clifford, Wynnie Richards-Thomas (pianist)

Programme included: Fickle Hearted Mimi (La Boheme) (with Grahame Clifford), Lend me your aid (Irene), Home to our mountains (Il Trovatore) (with Essie Ackland), E lucevan le stele (Tosca), Ch'ella mi creda libero (The Girl of the Golden West).

Travelling Opera Group (presented by the Arts Council of Great Britain) (10th to 12th October 1946) at the Bridgewater Arts Centre

Edgar Evans played the Centurion in the Ephesian Matron (Dibdin); Henry in the Faithful Centinel (Schubert), Basilio in The Marriage of Figaro (Mozart), the Milkman in The Policeman's Serenade (words by AP Herbert; music by Alfred Reynolds), Rudolph in La Boheme (Puccini) and Filch in The Beggar's Opera (Gay)..

Concert (Sunday 15th December 1946) at the Bournemouth Pavilion

Performers: Edgar Evans, Cecil White, The Municipal Orchestra

Programme included: Your tiny hand is frozen (La Boheme), 'Tis the day (Leoncavallo), 'Where my caravan has rested' (Lohr).

The Fairy Queen (Christmas 1946) at the Royal Opera House, Covent Garden
Edgar Evans played The God of the Birds (act I) and The Lover (Act II).
Performance conducted by Constant Lambert.

Manon (Tuesday 25th March 1947) at the Royal Opera House, Covent Garden
Edgar Evans played The Chevalier des Grieux.
Performance conducted by Reginald Goodall.

The Messiah (Thursday 10th April 1947) at the Victoria Hall, Hanley
Performers: Isobel Baillie, Kathleen Ferrier, Edgar Evans, Owen Brannigan, the Ceramic City Choir, conducted by Dr Malcolm Sargent.

Celebrity Concert (Sunday 4th May 1947) at the Odeon Theatre, Port Talbot
Performers: Ethel Gomer Lewis, Edgar Evans, Marian Nowakowski
Programme included: Flower Song (Carmen), E lucevan le stele (Tosca), Your tiny hand is frozen (La Boheme), Lovely Maid in the Moonlight (La Boheme) (with Ethel Gomer Lewis).

Celebrity Concert (Sunday 18th May 1947) at the Windsor Cinema, Neath
Performers: Blanche Turner, Edgar Evans, Bruce Dargavel.
Programme included: Lend me your aid (Irene), In This Solemn Hour (Force of Destiny) (with Bruce Dargavel), Your tiny hand is frozen (La Boheme), Lovely Maid in the Moonlight (La Boheme) (with Blanche Turner), E lucevan le stele (Tosca).

Turandot (Thursday 29th May 1947) at the Royal Opera House, Covent Garden
Edgar Evans played Pang, minister of the Princess Turandot.
Performance conducted by Constant Lambert.

● *Edgar as Pang (left) in the first production of Turandot at Covent Garden after the War.*

Der Rosenkavalier (Monday 18th August 1947) at the Theatre Royal, Glasgow

Edgar Evans played the Italian tenor and the Landlord.
Performance conducted by Karl Rankl.

Concert (Tuesday 2nd December 1947) at the Arts Centre, Bridgewater

Performers: The Bridgewater String Orchestra, Edgar Evans.

The Mastersingers (Wednesday 4th February 1948) at the Royal Opera House, Covent Garden

Edgar Evans played Vogelgesang, a furrier.
Performance conducted by Karl Rankl.

Tristan und Isolde (Thursday 19th February 1948) at the Royal Opera House, Covent Garden

Edgar Evans played a Young Seaman.
Performance conducted by Karl Rankl.

● *Edgar as Vogelgesang in The Mastersingers.*

124

The Liverpool Cymric Vocal Union's Annual Concert (Saturday 6th March 1948) at The Central Hall, Liverpool

Performers: The Liverpool Cymric Vocal Union, Mary Jarred, Edgar Evans

Programme included: Yr Hen Gerddor / The Old Minstrel (D Pughe Evans), Lend me your aid (Irene), To Music (Schubert), Songs My Mother Taught Me (Dvorak), 'Tis the Day (Leoncavallo), Home to our mountains (Il Trovatore) (with Mary Jarred).

Celebrity Concert (Easter Sunday 28th March 1948) at The Grand Pavilion, Llandrindod Wells

Performers: Edgar Evans, Joan Butler, WHJ Jenkins (violinist)

Programme included: Flower Song (Carmen), Gwlad y Delyn/Land of the Harp (John Henry), To Music (Schubert), Songs My Mother Taught Me (Dvorak), 'Tis the Day (Leoncavallo), Lovely Maid in the Moonlight (La Boheme) (with Joan Butler).

Boris Godunov (Wednesday 12th May 1948) at the Royal Opera House, Covent Garden

Edgar Evans played The Pretender, named Grigory, afterwards the false Dmitri (a novice in Pimen's cave).

Performance conducted by Karl Rankl.

Celebrity Concert (30th May 1948) at The Cherry Tree Ballroom, Welwyn Garden City

Performers: Edgar Evans, Bruce Dargavel, The Welwyn Garden City Male Voice Choir

Programme included: Flower Song (Carmen), Dream Song (Manon), In This Solemn Hour (Force of Destiny) (with Bruce Dargavel).

Concert by the Royal Opera (Saturday 10th July 1948) at Chester Cathedral

Performers: Blanche Turner, Edith Coates, Edgar Evans, Tom Williams, The Royal Opera Chorus.

Programme included: The Creation, parts I and II (Haydn), Church scene (The Mastersingers), Easter Hymn (Cavalleria Rusticana), excerpts from The Fairy Queen (Purcell), Hallelujah Chorus from The Messiah (Handel).

Music for the Millions (Sunday 11th July 1948) at the Pier Pavilion, Llandudno

Performers: The Covent Garden Opera Chorus, Edgar Evans, Tom Williams, Edith Coates, Blanche Turner.

Programme included: Dream Song (Manon), Lovely maid in the moonlight (La Boheme) (with Blanche Turner), Quartet (Rigoletto) (with Blanche Turner, Edith Coates and Tom Williams).

Celtic Concert (Sunday 8th August 1948) at the Grand Pavilion, Porthcawl

Performers: Laelia Finneberg, Edgar Evans, Meirion Williams (pianist)

Programme included: Gwlad y Delyn/Land of the Harp (John Henry), Cavatina of Spring Love (Leigh Henry), Yr Hen Gerddor / The Old Minstrel (D Pughe Evans), English Rose (Merrie England), Lovely Maid in the Moonlight (La Boheme) (with Laelia Finneberg).

Sacred Concert (Sunday 22nd August 1948) in Llanybydder

Performers: Blanche Turner, Edgar Evans, Idris Daniels

Programme included: Lend me your aid (Irene), In This Solemn Hour (Force of Destiny) (with Idris Daniels), Your Tiny Hand is Frozen (La Boheme), Miserere (Il Trovatore) (with Blanche Turner).

24th season of Celebrity Concerts (10th October 1948) at the Municipal Hall, Borough of Colne

Performers: Christina Carroll, Bessie Collins, Edgar Evans, Trevor Anthony.

Festival Lyra of Poetry and Music (Monday 23rd May 1949) at the Central Hall, Westminster

Performers: Margaret Rawlings, Richard Ainley, Mollie Davies, Edgar Evans, Gordon Holdom, Wilfred Worden, the London Welsh Women's Choir, the London Civic Symphony Orchestra.

Programme included: Gather ye rosebuds (William Lawes), I am confirmed (Henry Lawes), None shall sleep (Turandot), Cavatina of Spring Love (The Moon Robber).

Grand Concert (Sunday 21st August 1949) in Llanybydder

Performers: Zoe Cresswell, Edgar Evans, Howell Glynne, the Welsh National Opera Chorus.

Programme included: This Girl I've found you (The Bartered Bride) (with Howell Glynne), On with the Motley (Pagliacci), the Flower Song (Carmen), Trio and Finale (Faust) (with Zoe Cresswell and Howell Glynne).

Salome (Friday 11th November 1949) at the Royal Opera House, Covent Garden

Edgar Evans played Narraboth, a young Syrian, Captain of the Guard.

Performance conducted by Karl Rankl.

Boris Godunov (Saturday 19th November 1949) at the Royal Opera House, Covent Garden

Edgar Evans played the Pretender, named Grigory, afterwards the false Dmitri (a novice in Pimen's cave).

Performance conducted by Warwick Braithwaite.

St David's Day dinner and concert (1st March 1950) at the Polygon Hotel, Southampton

Performers: Edgar Evans, Ruby Copp.

La Traviata (Saturday 18th March 1950) at the Liverpool Empire

Edgar Evans played Armand Duval, friend of Gaston, a young man of fashion.

Performance conducted by Reginald Goodall.

A Grand Concert and Organ Recital (Tuesday 21st March 1950) at Walham Green Welsh Presbyterian Church, London SW6

Performers: Lyn Harry (organist), Edgar Evans.

Programme included: Lend me your aid (Irene), Yr Hen Gerddor / The Old Minstrel (D Pughe Evans), 'Largo' (Handel), Gwlad y Delyn / Land of the Harp (John Henry).

Carmen [and other pieces] (Saturday 25th March 1950) at the Town Hall, West Bromwich

Performers: Nina Barboné, Gita Denise, Edgar Evans, Stanley Mason.

Programme included – in addition to a concert version of Carmen – E lucevan le stele (Tosca), lend me your aid (Irene)

Das Rheingold (Monday 19th June 1950) at the Royal Opera House, Covent Garden (also broadcast on BBC Radio)

Edgar Evans played Froh.

Performance conducted by Karl Rankl.

A Harold Fielding Concert (Sunday 23rd July 1950) at the Winter Garden, Eastbourne

Performers: Joseph Cooper, Edgar Evans, Barbara Sumner, Kenneth Horne, Richard Murdoch.

Programme included: Lend me your aid (Irene), My Dreams (Tosti), E lucevan le stele (Tosca), O Maiden, my Maiden (Frederica).

The Flying Dutchman (Thursday 19th October 1950) at the Royal Opera House, Covent Garden

Edgar Evans played The Steersman of Daland's ship.

Performance conducted by Karl Rankl.

The Queen of Spades (Saturday 23rd December 1950) at the Royal Opera House, Covent Garden

Edgar Evans played Hermann, an officer in the Army.

Performance conducted by Erich Kleiber.

The Flying Dutchman (Monday 1st January 1951) at the Royal Opera House, Covent Garden

Edgar Evans played Erik, a Hunstman.

Performance conducted by Karl Rankl.

Salome (Thursday 25th January 1951) at the Royal Opera House, Covent Garden

Edgar Evans played Narraboth, a young Syrian, Captain of the

Guard.
Performance conducted by Karl Rankl.

Blodwen (Saturday 3rd March 1951) at the Kingsway Hall, London
Edgar Evans played Syr Hywel Ddu
Performance conducted by Morgan Jones.

Concert (Easter Sunday, 25th March 1951) at the Palladium, Aberdare
Performers: Patricia Martina Howard, Edgar Evans, The Nedd Singers, Glyn Neath.

Programme included: lend me your aid (Irene), E lucevan le stelle (Tosca), O Maiden, my Maiden (Frederica), the Flower Song (Carmen), My Dreams (Tosti).

Carmen (Sunday 15th April 1951) at St Andrew's Hall, Glasgow
Performers: Constance Shacklock, Victoria Elliott, Edgar Evans, Leyland White, Patrick Maher, Dorothy Roberton, May Brown, Reginald Glendinning, George Melville, the Glasgow Grand Opera Society, the Scottish National Orchestra, conductor Walter Susskind.

The Pilgrim's Progress (Thursday 26th April 1951 – first performance) at the Royal Opera House, Covent Garden
Edgar Evans played the Interpreter and A Celestial Messenger.
Performance conducted by Leonard Hancock.

Manon (Friday 1st June 1951) at the Royal Opera House, Covent Garden
Edgar Evans played The Chevalier des Grieux.
Performance conducted by Warwick Braithwaite.

Queen of Spades (Wednesday 14th November 1951) at the Royal Opera House, Covent Garden
Edgar Evans played Hermann, an officer of the Army.
Performance conducted by Vilem Tausky.

The Messiah (Thursday 29th November 1951) at the Welsh Tabernacl, King's Cross

Performers: Ena Mitchell, Netta Griffiths, Edgar Evans, Bruce Dargavel, the King's Cross Welsh Choral Society, conducted by Cyril Anthony.

Celebrity Concert (26th December 1951) at the Welfare Hall, Ystradgynlais

Performers: Blanche Turner, Edgar Evans, Maimie Williams, the Ystradgynlais Male Voice Choir.

Programme included: Lend me your aid (Irene), excerpts from Manon (Massenet), O loveliness beyond compare (The Magic Flute).

Turandot (Saturday 12th January 1952) at the Royal Opera House, Covent Garden

Edgar Evans played The Unknown Prince (Calaf), son of Timur.
Performance conducted by Sir John Barbirolli.

Wozzeck (Tuesday 22nd January 1952) at the Royal Opera House, Covent Garden

Edgar Evans played Andres.
Performance conducted by Erich Kleiber.

Grand Concert (Thursday 24th January 1952) at Y Tabernacl, King's Cross

Performers: Meirion Williams, Jennifer Vyvyan, Marian Nowakowski, Telynores Dwyryd, Edgar Evans.

Programme included: Lend me your aid (Irene), Lovely maid in the moonlight (La Boheme (with Jennifer Vyvyan), O loveliness beyond compare (The Magic Flute).

Billy Budd (Saturday 26th April 1952) at the Royal Opera House, Covent Garden

Edgar Evans played Captain Vere.
Performance conducted by Peter Gellhorn.

Fourth Sunday Popular Concert (27th April 1952) at the Royal Albert Hall

Performers: Victoria Sladen, Edgar Evans, the London Symphony Orchestra, conductor Walter Susskind.

Programme included: the Prize Song (Die Mastersinger von Nürnberg), E lucevan le stelle (Tosca).

Beethoven Choral Symphony (Monday 19th May 1952) at the Royal Opera House, Covent Garden

Performers: Sylvia Fisher, Constance Shacklock, Edgar Evans, Norman Walker, the Covent Garden Opera Chorus, The Covent Garden Orchestra, conducted by Erich Kleiber.

Das Rheingold (1952) at Rome Opera

Edgar Evans played Froh

Performance conducted by Erich Kleiber

Promenade Concert (Wednesday 2nd July 1952) at the Free Trade Hall, Manchester

Performers: The Hallé Orchestra conducted by George Weldon, Edgar Evans.

Programme included: Celesta Aida (Aida), Nessun Dorma (Turandot), Where'er you walk (Handel), Songs my mother taught me (Dvorak), I love thee (Grieg).

Concert (Friday 11th July 1952) at the Royal Hall, Harrogate

Performers: The Hallé Orchestra, conducted by Sir John Barbirolli, Edgar Evans.

Programme included: O Loveliness beyond compare (The Magic Flute), Il mio tesoro (Don Giovanni), Celeste Aida (Aida), Nessun Dorma (Turandot).

A Masked Ball (Thursday 23rd October 1952) at the Royal Opera House, Covent Garden

Edgar Evans played Gustavus III, King of Sweden (Riccardo).

Performance conducted by John Pritchard.

Boris Godunov (Tuesday 30th December 1952) at the Royal Opera House, Covent Garden

Edgar Evans played the Pretender, named Grigory, afterwards the false Dmitri (a novice in Pimen's cave).

Performance conducted by Issay Dobrowen.

La Boheme (Thursday 12th February 1953) at the Royal Opera House, Covent Garden

Edgar Evans played Rudolph, a poet.

Performance conducted by Sir John Barbirolli.

Celebrity Concert (Wednesday 25th February 1953) at St Martin's Church Hall, Caerphilly

Performers: Grace Howell-Wilson, Edgar Evans, The Caerphilly Ladies' Choir, the Pontypridd Male Glee Singers.

Programme included: Lend me your aid (Irene), Home to our mountains (It Trovatore) (with Grace Howell-Wilson), E lucevan le stelle (Tosca), None shall sleep (Turandot), the Flower Song (Carmen)

Elektra (Wednesday 13th May 1953) at the Royal Opera House, Covent Garden

Edgar Evans played Aegisth.

Performance conducted by Erich Kleiber.

Wozzeck (Thursday 21st May 1953) at the Royal Opera House, Covent Garden

Edgar Evans played Andres.

Performance conducted by Erich Kleiber.

A Grand Coronation Concert (Sunday 21st June 1953) at the Workmen's Hall, Tredegar

Performers: The Tredegar Orpheus Male Voice Choir, Edgar Evans, Bruce Dargavel.

Programme included: O loveliness beyond compare (The Magic Flute), the Flower Song (Carmen), None shall sleep (Turandot).

La Boheme (Monday 3rd August 1953) at the Theatre Royal, Bulawayo, Rhodesia

Edgar Evans played Rudolph, a poet.

Performance conducted by Sir John Barbirolli.

Celebrity Concert (Wednesday 7th October 1953) at The Belgian Institute, London

Performers: Elizabeth Hawes, Edgar Evans, Sheila Randell, Howell Glynne, Leslie French.

Programme included: Lend me your aid (Irene), 'Welsh Melody, Nessun Dorma (Turandot), Duet (The Force of Destiny) (with Howell Glynne)

Tredegar Orpheus Male Voice Party – Annual Celebrity Concert (Wednesday 14th October 1953)

Soloists: Victoria Elliott and Edgar Evans.

Programme included: Lend me your aid (Irene), O weep no more, Liu (Turandot), Violetta and Alfred (La Traviata) (with Victoria Elliott), E lucevan le stelle (Tosca).

Salome (Thursday 29th October 1953) at the Royal Opera House, Covent Garden

Edgar Evans played Narraboth, a young Syrian, Captain of the Guard.

Performance conducted by Rudolf Kempe.

A Masked Ball (Saturday 31st October 1953) at the Royal Opera House, Covent Garden

Edgar Evans played Gustavus III, King of Sweden (Riccardo).

Performance conducted by John Pritchard.

Peter Grimes (Friday 20th November 1953) at the Royal Opera House, Covent Garden

Edgar Evans played Peter Grimes, a fisherman.

Performance conducted by Reginald Goodall.

Carmen (Saturday 12th December 1953) at the Royal Opera House, Covent Garden

Edgar Evans played Don Jose, a corporal.
Performance conducted by John Pritchard.

Turandot (Wednesday 13th January 1954) at the Royal Opera House, Covent Garden

Edgar Evans played the unknown Prince (Calaf), son of Timur.
Performance conducted by Vilem Tausky

Fortieth annual concert, in aid of the Leeds Jewish Board of Guardians (Sunday 17th January 1954) at the Theatre Royal, Leeds

Performers: Allan Schiller, Jack L Puttnam, Mary Millar, Dorothy Marno, Benny Hill, The Gaunt Brothers, Edgar Evans, John Cameron.

Programme included: E lucevan le stelle (Tosca), O Maiden, my Maiden (Frederica), Lend me your aid (Irene), O sole mio.

Grand Concert (Thursday 21st January 1954) at Y Tabernacl, King's Cross

Performers: Meirion Williams, Decima Morgan-Lewis, Bruce Dargavel, Triawd Llanuwchllyn (a trio singing in the 'penillion' style), Edgar Evans.

Programme included: Where'er you walk (Handel), the Flower Song (Carmen), Fickle-hearted Mimi (La Boheme) (with Bruce Dargavel), Ah! Be gone vision fair (Manon), None shall sleep (Turandot).

Great Annual Concert organised by the Polish Ex-Combatants' Association (Sunday 31st January 1954) at St George's Hall, Bradford

Performers: Marian Nowakowski, J Sulikowski, Edgar Evans, Janina Wtorzecka.

Programme included: Lend me your aid (Irene), None shall sleep (Turandot), If I pray (Gounod) (with Marian Nowakowski).

Madam Butterfly (Saturday 27th February 1954) at the Davis Theatre, Croydon

Edgar Evans played Lieutenant F B Pinkerton, US Navy.

Performance conducted by Emanuel Young.

Der Freischütz (Friday 26th March 1954) at the Palace Theatre, Manchester

Edgar Evans played Max, a young forester in the service of Prince Ottokar.

Performance conducted by Edward Downes.

International Maifestspiele Wiesbaden (1st -26th May 1954)

8th May & 9th May: Peter Grimes

The Royal Covent Garden Opera, London

Conductor: Reginald Goodall.

Producer: Tyrone Guthrie.

Principal singers: Coates, Fisher, Jacopi, Mills, Turner, Davies, Donlevy, Evans, Glynne, Kraus, Lanigan, Nilsson.

This is Show Business (31st May 1954), broadcast on BBC Television

Performers: Eric Barker, Frances Day, Brian Reece, Freddie Sales, Pierre Bel; Dennis Brain; Edgar Evans.

Programme included: Nessun Dorma (Turandot)

Carmen (Tuesday 13th July 1954) at the Royal Opera House, Covent Garden

Edgar Evans played Don Jose, a corporal.

Performance conducted by John Pritchard.

Wozzeck (Wednesday 3rd November 1954) at the Royal Opera House, Covent Garden

Edgar Evans played The Drum Major.

Performance conducted by Reginald Goodall.

The Tales of Hoffmann (Saturday 20th November 1954) at the Royal Opera House, Covent Garden

Edgar Evans played Hoffmann, a poet.

Performance conducted by Edward Downes.

Der Freischütz (Wednesday 22nd December 1954) at the Royal Opera House, Covent Garden

Edgar Evans played Max, a young forester in the service of Prince Ottokar.

Performance conducted by Edward Downes.

Grand Celebrity Concert (Friday 14th January 1955) at Peniel, Aberayron

Performers: Mary Jones, Edgar Evans, Bruce Dargavel, Jennie Davies.

Programme included: Through the Woodland, through the Meadow (Der Freischutz), None shall sleep (Turandot), Lovely maid in the moonlight (La Boheme) (with Mary Jones), In this solemn hour (La Forza del destino) (with Bruce Dargavel), the Flower Song (Carmen), Holy Angels (Faust) (with Mary Jones and Bruce Dargavel).

Salome (7th July 1955) at the Royal Opera House, Covent Garden, and broadcast live on the BBC

Edgar Evans played Narraboth, a Syrian captain.

Performance conducted by Rudolf Kempe.

The Queen of Spades (Monday 14h May 1956) at the Royal Opera House, Covent Garden

Edgar Evans played Hermann, an officer in the Army.

Performance conducted by Rafael Kubelik.

Das Rheingold (Thursday 24th May 1956) at the Royal Opera House, Covent Garden

Edgar Evans played Froh.

Performance conducted by Rudolf Kempe.

Grand Concert (21st June 1956) at the Royal National Eisteddfod, Llangefni

Performers: Nancy Thomas, Edgar Evans, Cymdeithas Gorawl Llangefni a'r Cylch (choir).

Programme included: Yr Hen Gerddor / The Old Minstrel (D Pughe Evans), O na byddai'n haf o hyd/ O that summer stayed for e'er (William Davies), Lend me your aid (Irene), the Flower Song (Carmen).

The Radio Show (Wednesday 22nd August 1956) at Earl's Court and broadcast on BBC Television

Edgar Evans officially opened the Radio Show by singing 'On with the Motley' (Pagliacci).

Jenufa (Monday 10th December 1956) at the Royal Opera House, Covent Garden

Edgar Evans played Steva Buryja, grandson and heir of Grandmother Buryja and step-brother of Laca.

Performance conducted by Rafael Kubelik.

Ruth (Thursday 20th June 1957) in the Jubilee Hall, Aldeburgh

Edgar Evans played Boaz.

Performance conducted by Charles Mackerras.

Turandot (Friday 12th July 1957) at the Royal Opera House, Covent Garden

Edgar Evans played the unknown Prince (Calaf), son of Timur.

Performance conducted by Rafael Kubelik.

Il Trovatore (24th October 1957) on BBC Television

Edgar Evans played Manrico.

Performance produced by Patricia Foy and conducted by Vic Oliver.

An Operatic Concert (Thursday 28th November 1957) at the Royal Albert Hall

Performers: Jacqueline Delman, Amy Shuard, Edgar Evans, Dennis

Noble, David Galliver, Jess Walters.

Programme included: excerpts from The Mastersingers, The Olympians, Aida.

Edgar Evans played Walther, a young knight from Franconia (The Mastersingers), Bacchus (The Olympians), Radames, Captain of the Guard (Aida).

Performance conducted by Sir Malcolm Sargent.

Don Carlos (Friday 9th May 1958) at the Royal Opera House, Covent Garden

Edgar Evans played the Count of Lerma, a Spanish nobleman

Performance conducted by Carlo Maria Giulini.

Hoffnung Interplanetary Music Festival (Friday 21st November and Saturday 22nd November 1958) – including 'Let's Fake An Opera' - at the Royal Festival Hall

An evening devised by Gerard Hoffnung, aided and abetted by John Amis, Malcolm Arnold, Ernest Bean, Colin Graham, Ian Hunter, Lawrence Leonard, David McBain, Humphrey Searle and Eric Thompson with Dame Edith Evans, The Hoffnung Festival opera Company and Chorus, the Hoffnung (alias Morley College) Symphony Orchestra, conducted by Norman Del Mar, the Band & Trumpeters of the Royal Military School of Music, the Dolmetsch Ensemble and John Amis, Malcolm Arnold, Jonathan Ashby, Francis Baines, Ernest Bean, Owen Brannigan, April Cantelo, Edith Coates, Joseph Cooper, Aaron Copland, Jacqueline Delman, John Dobson, Edgar Evans, Peter Glossop, Gerard Hoffnung, Joseph Horovitz, Otakar Krause, Gloria Lane, Elizabeth Poston, Sheila Rix, Duncan Robertson, Lionel Slater, Matyas Seiber, Ian Wallace.

Salome (Wednesday 28th January 1959) at the Royal Opera House, Covent Garden

Edgar Evans played Narraboth, a young Syrian, Captain of the Guard.

Performance conducted by Reginald Goodall.

Hoffnung Interplanetary Music Festival (Friday 6th February 1959) – including 'Let's Fake An Opera' - at the Royal Festival Hall

An evening devised by Gerard Hoffnung, aided and abetted by John Amis, Malcolm Arnold, Ernest Bean, Colin Graham, Ian Hunter, Lawrence Leonard, David McBain, Humphrey Searle and Eric Thompson with Dame Edith Evans, The Hoffnung Festival opera Company and Chorus, the Hoffnung (alias Morley College) Symphony Orchestra, conducted by Norman Del Mar, the Band & Trumpeters of the Royal Military School of Music, the Dolmetsch Ensemble and John Amis, Malcolm Arnold, Jonathan Ashby, Francis Baines, Ernest Bean, Thetis Blacker, Owen Brannigan, April Cantelo, Edith Coates, John Dobson, Edgar Evans, Peter Glossop, Rose Hill, Gerard Hoffnung, Jospeh Horovitz, Otakar Krause, Judith Pearce, Elizabeth Poston, Sheila Rix, Duncan Robertson, Lionel Slater, Matyas Seiber, Walter Todds, Ian Wallace.

Family Favourites (Thursday 25th June 1959) at the Leas Cliff Hall, Folkestone

Performers: Nina Walker, Edgar Evans, Michael Langdon.

Programme included: lend me your aid (Irene), To Music (Schubert), E lucevan le stelle (Tosca), Mattinata (Leoncavallo), Watchman! What of the night? (Sarjeant) (with Michael Langdon), Through the Woodland, through the Meadow (Der Freischutz), Songs my mother taught me (Dvorak), Ch'ella mi creda (La Fanciulla del West), This Girl I've found you (The Bartered Bride) (with Michael Langdon).

Das Rheingold (Friday 18th September 1959) at the Royal Opera House, Covent Garden

Edgar Evans played Froh.

Performance conducted by Franz Konwitschny.

Boris Godunov (Thursday 5th November 1959) at the Royal Opera House, Covent Garden

Edgar Evans played the Pretender, named Grigory, afterwards the false Dmitri (a novice in Pimen's cave).

Performance conducted by Jaroslav Krombholc.

Salome (Friday 13th November 1959) at the Royal Opera House, Covent Garden

Edgar Evans played Narraboth, a young Syrian, Captain of the Guard.
Performance conducted by Rudolf Kempe.

Aelwyd y Gân – a BBC TV weekly music programme (22nd January 1960) broadcast live from the British Nylon Spinners Clubhouse, Mamhilad

Performers: The BBC Welsh Orchestra, conducted by Arwel Hughes, The Beaufort Male Voice Choir, Heather Harper, Edgar Evans, Osian Ellis (harpist).

Programme included: Vesti la Giubba (Pagliacci).

St David's Day Celebration Concert (Thursday 3rd March 1960) at Brangwyn Hall, Swansea

Performers: Helen Watts, Edgar Evans, D Francgon Thomas (cellist), Mary Kendall (piano), Maselton and District Male Voice Choir, Brynmawr Welsh Folk Dancers, Parti Cerdd-dant Pontrhydyfen, Mynyddbach School Choir.

Programme included: Baner Ein Gwlad (Parry), Gwlad y Delyn (Henry), E lucevan le stelle (Tosca), Vesti la Giubba (Pagliacci).

The Trojans (Monday 2nd May 1960) at the Royal Opera House, Covent Garden

Edgar Evans played Helenus, son of Priam.
Performance conducted by John Matheson (and produced by John Gielgud).

Das Rheingold (Friday 16th September 1960) at the Royal Opera House, Covent Garden

Edgar Evans played Froh.
Performance conducted by Rudolf Kempe.

Peter Grimes (Thursday 17th November 1960) at the Royal Opera House, Covent Garden

Edgar Evans played Bob Boles, a Methodist fisherman.
Performance conducted by Meredith Davies.

Boris Godunov (Thursday 1st June 1961) at the Royal Opera House, Covent Garden

Edgar Evans played the Pretender, named Grigory, afterwards the false Dmitri (a novice in Pimen's cave).

Performance conducted by Reginald Goodall.

Boris Godunov (Saturday 10th June 1961) at the Royal Opera House, Covent Garden and broadcast live on the BBC

Edgar Evans played the Pretender, named Grigory, afterwards the false Dmitri (a novice in Pimen's cave).

Performance conducted by Reginald Goodall.

Grand Concert (Sunday 20th January 1963) at the Grand Theatre, Leeds

Performers: The Grand Theatre Orchestra, Inia Te Wiata, Roberta Desti, Norman George (violinist), Gill & Terry (guitars), John Bainton, Edgar Evans, Tommy Reilly (harmonica), Peter Goodwright.

Grand Concert (Thursday 24th January 1963) at the 'Jewin' Presbyterian Chapel, London

Performers: Edgar Evans, Eleanor Dwyryd, Elizabeth Vaughan, Gerwyn Morgan.

Programme included: Lend me your aid (Irene), Where'er you walk (Handel).

Sunbury and District Welsh Society Celebrity Concert (Thursday 17th October 1963) at The Sunbury Grammar School

Performers: Edgar Evans and the Gwalia Girl Singers.

Katerina Ismailova (Lady Macbeth of the Mtensk District) (Monday 2nd December 1963) at the Royal Opera House, Covent Garden

Edgar Evans played Zinovy Borisovich Ismailov.

Performance conducted by Edward Downes.

Billy Budd (Thursday 16th January 1964) at the Royal Opera House, Covent Garden

Edgar Evans played Captain Vere.
Performance conducted by Georg Solti.

The Messiah (Handel) (Saturday 25th January 1964) at the Tabernacle Chapel, Morriston, Swansea

Performers: Marion Studholme, Jean Allister, Edgar Evans, John Holmes, The Tabernacle Augmented Choir.
Performance conducted by EH Hughson.

Wozzeck (Thursday 29th October 1964) at the Royal Opera House, Covent Garden

Edgar Evans played The Drum Major.
Performance conducted by John Pritchard.

Die Meistersinger von Nürnberg (Friday 24th January 1969) at the Royal Opera House, Covent Garden

Edgar Evans played Moser, a tailor.
Performance conducted by Georg Solti.

Victory (Monday 13th April 1970) – first performance - at the Royal Opera House, Covent Garden

Edgar Evans played Captain Davidson.
Performance conducted by Edward Downes.

Parsifal (Wednesday 21st April 1971) at the Royal Opera House, Covent Garden

Edgar Evans played The First Knight.
Performance conducted by Reginald Goodall.

The Visit of the Old Lady (2nd June 1973) at Glyndebourne and broadcast on BBC Radio Three

Edgar Evans played the Butler.
Performance conducted by John Pritchard.

Also:

Grand Celebrity Concert (undated, 1950s?) at the Palace Theatre, Ebbw Vale

Performers: Blanche Turner, Edgar Evans.

Programme included: None shall sleep (Turandot), When the stars were brightly shining (Tosca), O loveliness beyond compare (The Magic Flute), duet (Manon) (with Blanche Turner).

From The Royal Opera House Annual Report 1957/58:

Aida: 16 performances, average paid attendance: 2,034

La Boheme: 4 performances, average paid attendance: 1,517

The Carmelites: 9 performances, average paid attendance: 1,428

Carmen: 24 performances, average paid attendance: 1,773 [Don Jose: Edgar Evans / Johnston / Nilsson / Vickers]

Elektra: 4 performances, average paid attendance: 1,834 (Aegisth: Edgar Evans]

Madam Butterfly: 5 performances, average paid attendance: 2,167

The Magic Flute: 5 performances, average paid attendance: 1,237

The Marriage of Figaro: 10 performances, average paid attendance: 1,544

A Masked Ball: 10 performances, average paid attendance: 1,277

Otello: 5 performances, average paid attendance: 1,693

Peter Grimes: 5 performances, average paid attendance: 1,544 [Peter Grimes: Edgar Evans / Pears]

Rigoletto: 12 performances, average paid attendance: 1,186

Der Ring Des Nibelungen (two cycles, average paid attendance for each performance: 2,079

Die Walkurie: one extra performance, paid attendance: 2,069

Götterdämmerung: 2 extra performances, average paid attendance: 1,939

The Tales of Hoffmann: 13 performances, average paid attendance: 1,403 [Hoffmann: Edgar Evans / Johnston]

Tosca: 7 performances, average paid attendance: 1,907

The Trojans: 8 performances, average paid attendance: 2,030

Il Trovatore: 4 performances, average paid attendance: 1,526

Turandot: 6 performances, average paid attendance: 1,632 [Calaf: Edgar Evans / Johnston / Midgley]

Appendix Three: the official story

Condensed from 'Opera at Covent Garden', an article which appeared in 'A Review 1946 – 1956'.

When, after the war, the decision was taken to re-open the Royal Opera House, Covent Garden, and run it as a national lyric theatre for opera and ballet, the Covent Garden Opera Trust, which had just been set up under the chairmanship of Lord Keynes, had to consider what its operatic policy would be. The trustees possessed two invaluable assets: the theatre itself and its operatic tradition.

The theatre had been secured by prompt action by Messrs Boosey and Hawkes Ltd, who acquired a short lease of the property in 1945 with a view to saving it for opera and ballet and ending its use as a dance hall. Boosey and Hawkes not only defrayed the preliminary expenses of the Covent Garden Committee, a body which preceded the Trust, but, in addition to the rent and rates of the building, they undertook to pay certain managerial salaries and the running expenses of the building. This arrangement was modified from time to time and ended in 1949.

The Opera House dates from 1858. The original theatre had been built by John Rich in 1732 out of the profits of The Beggar's Opera and, for over 100 years, Covent Garden functioned as one of London's two Royal Patent theatres. In 1847, the management decided to concentrate on operas to the exclusion of plays and advertised itself as the 'Royal Italian Opera'. By the end of the century, the word

'Italian' was dropped and it was styled as 'The Royal Opera, Covent Garden'.

In the autumn of 1945, the Covent Garden Opera Trust, had to choose between continuing the polyglot tradition of importing international artists or training a native company that would base its work on a repertory of foreign opera in translation – to establish a 'national style of operatic representation'. The Trust chose the latter course.

The Opera Company's first nine years fall into two periods. Karl Rankl was appointed musical director for opera in 1946 and held this position until he resigned to take up symphonic work in 1951. The following four years – until the appointment of Rafael Kubelik as musical director in 1955 – made considerable use of guest conductors as well as conductors on the Opera House's musical staff.

To Rankl fell the difficult task of forming the Opera Company and training it. In the summer of 1946, auditions were held all over England, Scotland and Wales. By 12th December, the company was strong enough for its chorus and some of its principals to appear with the Sadler's Wells Ballet in an adaptation – made by Constant Lambert - of Purcell's The Fairy Queen. The company made its first independent appearance on 14th January 1947 in Carmen.

Throughout the period under review [1946 – 1956], the executive control of the Opera House's affairs has been in the hands of David Webster, who brought to his task the experience he had gained as a businessman and chairman of the Liverpool Philharmonic Society.

In the course of the company's first nine years, 46 operas were produced, six of them for the first time on any stage. They have been drawn from the following repertoires:

German	18	Italian	11
English	9	French	4
Russian	3	Czechoslovakian	1

Thirty of these productions were mounted in the first five years when Karl Rankl was the musical director; 14 during the four years' interregnum, and the remaining two during the first months of Rafael Kubelik's appointment. It was necessary to build up a repertory as quickly as possible – most of the important foreign opera houses have a stock of some 60 works – but the pace set during the first few years at Covent Garden was fierce and put a great strain on the company.

All these operas were produced in translation, with the exceptions of Norma, Otello, Der Ring des Nibelungen, Tristan und Isolde, Parsifal and Elektra.

The singers in the company work for some 42 weeks of the year. They are contracted exclusively to the Opera House and perform elsewhere only with the Opera House's permission. It is an advantage of the system that some control can be kept over the number of times singers perform, the smaller parts can sometimes be sung by leading singers and substitutes are usually available in case of illness. All this makes for a generally high level of ensemble.

That the methods employed had successful results was shown by the production of Der Rosenkavalier in the spring of 1947 and, later, by that of Wozzeck in 1952. No member of the company had ever sung in Der Rosenkavalier before and the work was also new to members of the orchestra. Nevertheless, it was generally agreed that the production was of a high standard and this was equally true of the production of Wozzeck which is notoriously one of the most difficult operas in the repertory. The Covent Garden production in 1952 was the first ever undertaken in Great Britain.

Credit for the styeady improvement in musical standards must go to the guest conductors as well as the resident musical staff. Of native conductors, special mention should be made of Sir Thomas Beecham, whose performances of The Mastersingers and The Bohemian Girl renewed an important link with the Covent Garden seasons of pre-war days. The first foreign conductor the company engaged was Erich Kleiber, under whose direction the company gave some of its best performances of Elektra, Der Rosenkavalier and Wozzeck.

The same pattern has been followed where production is concerned. Peter Brook was resident producer from January 1948 to February 1950 and was succeeded by Christopher West.

Care has been taken in choosing designers. Special mention should be made of Leslie Hurry (Turandot and Der Ring des Nibelungen), Oliver Messel (The Queen of Spades and The Magic Flute), Georges Wakhevitch (Boris Godunov, The Tales of Hoffmann, Otello and Carmen) and Caspar Neher (Wozzeck).

Touring is not a recognised part of most foreign opera companies but the Royal Opera undertakes tours – usually for eight weeks in the spring – paying visits to Birmingham, Cardiff, Coventry, Croydon, Edinburgh, Glasgow, Leeds, Liverpool and Manchester. In 1953, on the occasion of the Rhodes Centenary celebrations the company went as far afield as Central Africa, visiting Bulawayo and taking four operas with them.

A number of short visits have been paid to towns in Europe. Peter Grimes was played at the Théâtre de la Monnaie, Brussels, and the Opéra, Paris, (June 1948) and at the Wiesbaden Festival (May 1954), while Billy Budd was taken to the Théâtre des Champs Elysees, Paris, for the Festival of Twentieth Century Art (May 1952).

Appendix Four: the technique and the art of singing

The art of singing is either extremely simple or extremely complex. Almost everyone can sing – so singing is simple - but not everyone can sing well.

Traditionally, the art of singing involves being able to make the right sounds at the right volume and at the right time. Making these sounds involves the skill of being able to hear correctly and to reproduce a sound faithfully but there are other skills involved in being able to sing well.

This is the province of the technique of singing. It is important for singers to have a good technique in order to augment and enhance their art.

The act of singing involves taking in air into the lungs, then passing that air – in a controlled way – over the voice box and, from there, via an 'open' (or relaxed) throat into the mouth. Taking air into our lungs is something we all do – unthinkingly – many times a day. Nonetheless, there is an art to taking in the optimum amount of air in order to use it in voice production – both in singing and speaking.

It is important to breathe 'from the diaphragm'. This is best illustrated by observing the singer. When breathing in, the shoulders should remain immobile while the abdomen should push out (because the whole of the lungs are inflating). This is sometimes called 'breathing from the bottom of the lungs'. When a person gasps for air

– for example after a period of hard physical exertion – their shoulders will rise and fall as they pant. Here, their lungs are working inefficiently, just taking in short gasps of air to meet an immediate need for oxygen. It is the response of fear or panic ('I've not got enough air!'). If singers breathe in short gasps – characterised by raising their shoulders – they will not have enough air to perform.

Having taken in enough air, its exhalation needs to be controlled – ensuring that you keep enough air in reserve in the lungs to keep the 'pressure' or 'energy' in the voice. Passing this air over the vocal chords produces sound but this sound must be both refined and amplified.

In order to amplify the sound, you have to create as large an area inside the mouth as possible in order to allow the sound waves being created to resonate. A small space will only produce a relatively small sound, while a larger space will produce a larger sound.

However, amplification is only a part of the sound production process. The sound must be 'focused' in order to produce what has been variously called the 'buzz', 'ping' or 'metallic quality' in a voice. Not only does this quality make a voice sound 'alive' and full of energy, it also enables it to be heard over a large and noisy orchestra.

There are different schools of thought about how to produce this focus. The English way is to make use of the nasal passages – the sinuses – either side of the nose. Placing the voice in these will produce a 'ring' in the voice but the result will be a 'confined sound' which, unless the singer is careful, could also migrate to the nose and produce the nasal sound that every singer tries hard not to cultivate and audiences never want to hear.

The Italian way to produce this quality in the voice is to 'place' the voice against the hard palate in the mouth. If the hard palate is thought of as a drum, the Italian way to sing is to place the sound against the drum, while the English way is to place the sound inside the drum. Placing the voice in the Italian way allows it to resonate in an 'unconfined' way and helps to add a 'freedom' to the voice that many people find exciting and thrilling.

The hard palate is what can be felt by running the tip of your tongue backwards from the top of your teeth to the top of your mouth. When the tip of your tongue cannot go further back in your mouth, you have reached the soft palate (more of that later). Since it is important to (a) feel in control of the sound you are making and (b) to direct this sound forwards – towards your audience – the optimum place on the hard palate to 'place' the voice is at the front of the hard palate: just a little way above your top front teeth.

This provides a safe 'anchor' for the voice. However, this will only work if you have the maximum space in your mouth – in order to allow the sound you are making from your vocal chords to resonate and amplify itself. This is where the soft palate comes in.

Every time we yawn, our soft palates rise – in order to allow in the maximum amount of air, since a yawn is our body's way of telling us that we do not have enough oxygen to keep our body operating properly.

A singer cultivates the skill of raising the soft palate for two main reasons: it allows the singer to take in more air than would otherwise have been the case and, perhaps more importantly, it facilitates maximum amplification of produced sound as well as contributing towards producing 'rounded' vowel sounds.

Moreover, it prevents singers straining their throats. Placing the voice on the hard palate without creating 'space' inside the mouth via raising the palate leaves the air with nowhere to resonate, so not only will a smaller than necessary sound be produced but some of the energy involved in the voice production will go backwards and damage the vocal chords.

There is a point in a singer's voice where it is impossible for the singer to sing higher without 'changing' the way s/he produces the note. Italians know this as the 'passagio' and define it as when the 'chest' voice moves into the 'head' voice. The key to being a singer is to be able to move from the 'chest' to the 'head' voice without the listeners knowing that such a transition has occurred.

This 'break' in the voice will happen around B or B natural for a bass; D or D sharp for a baritone; D sharp for a mezzo; E or E sharp for a soprano, and F or F sharp for a tenor. The actual note on which this change needs to occur will depend upon the individual characteristics of each voice – for example, how 'light' or 'heavy' it is, as well as the inherent 'quality' of the voice.

It is impossible to move through this 'break' in the voice successfully without lifting the soft palate – while still keeping the voice focused, or anchored, to the hard palate. Singing these higher notes without raising the soft palate not only quickly tires the voice but also strains the vocal chords. Consequently, the singer can never be sure of reaching these notes in performance and will have a foreshortened singing career.

However, once you have mastered this technique, you will be able to sing the higher notes in your vocal register either loud or mezzo voce. It is here that the singer needs a mentor or vocal coach – rather than a repetiteur who will be able to teach the singer to sing songs. This mentor or vocal coach needs to be a specialist in the technique of singing and a good listener – to listen critically to the sounds that the singer makes and then be able to offer positive suggestions on how to improve those sounds.

The final piece in the jigsaw that is the technique of singing is the forming of the sounds that become words. In particular, it is important to cultivate a 'line' in singing, a 'roundness of tone' and to sing vowels correctly - particularly: (a) ah; (e) eh; (i) i and (o) oh. This can be helped by creating space in the mouth – raising the soft palate – and 'thinking high'. Various teachers try to convey this by suggesting that the singer thinks that s/he is looking down on the whole process and acting the part of a noble, with all its attendant poise and demeanor.

Another way of getting the soft palate to rise (a way advocated by Gerald Davies) is to sing or say - with 'received pronunciation' - 'Glah'.

The next – and highly important – stage is the position of the lips. The shape of the lips governs the ultimate sound. The tongue has nothing to do with the process of singing – in the sense that it will automatically adopt the correct shape to produce the sound shaped by the lips.

Since the volume and resonance ('ping') of the sound is being made inside the mouth, the job of the lips is to give meaning to that sound and allow it to escape into the world. Just as water pressure increases the smaller the aperture through which it passes, so the lips need to both shape the words and contain the sounds of the singer.

A mouth that is too open will not deliver the crispness of sound required. Of course, the size of the aperture of the lips will depend on the pitch of the note relative to the vocal range of the singer, as well as the requirements of the song being sung.

Some songs require all the words to be carefully enunciated – perhaps at speed – as in the 'factotum' aria in 'The Barber of Seville' or in any of the 'patter songs' in the Gilbert & Sullivan canon. Here, the singer will need to gather – almost purse – the lips to give a rapid and precise delivery. Other songs require a vowel-rich legato, where speed of delivery comes second to making a beautiful sound – the meaning of the term 'bel canto'. Here, the singer is required to produce equally rounded vowel sounds throughout the piece. In such songs, much is made of the 'line' that the song demands. Of course, all songs demand – to some degree or other - that the singer keeps a 'line' throughout the song. This is what makes the song an entity in itself and intelligible to an audience. It also demonstrates that part of the singer's art that is concerned with 'putting over' or performing a song.

It is here that a vocal coach is of most help to a singer wishing to understand not only how a particular song is usually sung but also how to perform it 'properly' while bringing something of their own interpretation to it, which is the essence of art in singing. That said, art can only exist in singing because technique is also present. Once that technique is an almost unconscious part of the singer's life – like breathing is to almost everyone – then the singer can work on perfecting her/his art.

● *Edgar, putting his singing technique to good use as Don Jose in Carmen, with Constance Shacklock.*

Appendix Five: The Edgar Evans file - some key documents

Sadler's Wells

ROSEBERY AVENUE. E.C.1.

IN CONJUNCTION WITH THE OLD VIC, S.E.1.

LESSEE & MANAGER - - - - LILIAN BAYLIS, C.H., M.A., OXON. (HON)., LL.D., BIRM. (HON.)

HON. TREASURER
SIR REGINALD ROWE.

ACTING MANAGER:
EDWARD HOLBROOK.

ALL COMMUNICATIONS WITH
REGARD TO ARTISTES AND
PRODUCTIONS SHOULD BE
ADDRESSED TO OLD VIC.

TELEPHONES:
CLERKENWELL 1121-1122 BOX OFFICE.
TERMINUS 2233 ACTING MANAGER.
CLERKENWELL 6215 STAGE DOOR.

May 27th. 1937

Dear Mr. Evans,

I am enclosing herewith contract accepted by you in your letter
of the 23rd. Will you please sign and return the duplicate copy?
If you call here next week our librarian, Mr. Cornish, will ~~~~
~~~~ to give you the neccessary scores.

Metropolitan Police.

1429

This is to certify that _Timothy Edgar Evans,_

"_S_" Division, joined the Metropolitan Police War Reserve in a full-time, paid capacity,

on the _2nd_ day of _September,_ 19_39_, and resigned his

situation on the _5th_ day of _June,_ 194_2_, _having been_

discharged on account of ill health.

He performed his duties satisfactorily and the Commissioner appreciates the services he

rendered to the Metropolitan Police during the above period.

Given under my Hand and Seal .... _for Commissioner
of Police
Deputy Assistant Commissioner._ ⎰ _of the Metropolis._

METROPOLITAN POLICE OFFICE,
NEW SCOTLAND YARD, S.W.1.

_24th_ _day of_ _June,_ 194_2_.

Wembley Police (District) Garage Athletic Club

President : Supt. D. W. ELSLEY

WEMBLEY DISTRICT GARAGE, RANELAGH ROAD, WEMBLEY

WEMBLEY 1844-5 ....5th. June................ 1950.

Dear Sir,

     I have been asked by my colleagues of the above
Club to say how much we appreciated your grand performance
at our Smoking Concert on Wednesday 24th. May 1950.
     Words fail me when I endeavour to express the
pleasure you gave us, but you can rest assured that the
applause given by all was well and truly meant.
     With best wishes for the future,

           Believe me,

             Yours Sincerely.

              (Benjamin Mills)

              Social Secretary.

154

Royal Opera House

COVENT GARDEN LONDON WC2

Telephone: Temple Bar 8811   Telegrams: Amidstrand

8.4.'46.

Dear *Mr Evans*,

    A preliminary audition will
be held here on next Monday, April 15th
at which representatives of the Covent
would like to hear you sing.

    Will you please let me know,
by return if possible, whether you
intend being present, in which case please
come to the Stage Door at *11.35 a.m.* .

    An accompanist will be
provided.

Yoursfaithfully,
pp ADMINISTRATION

(Miss) Josephine O'Donnell

Royal Opera House

COVENT GARDEN LONDON WC2

Telephone: Temple Bar 8811   Telegrams: Amidstrand

31st July,1946.

Dear Mr.Evans,

I have spoken to Dr.Rankl
and told him of your engagement dates
with the **Arts** Council and of your
request to sing again for Covent Garden
before you take up that work on Oct.1st
He hopes to hear you some time in Sept.
and has asked me to remind him of it.

Yours sincerely,

Josephine O'Donnell

I hope you have a very nice holiday;
I am off to Ireland myself on the 9th
for three weeks.

Edgar Evans, Esq.,
21, Adelaide Road,
Hampstead, N.W.3.

Royal Opera House

COVENT GARDEN LONDON WC2

Telephone: Temple Bar 8811   Telegrams: Amidstrand

14th August 1946.

Dear Mr. Evans,

We would like you to come and work for us at Covent Garden and I would like to have an opportunity of discussing the whole thing with you in the near future.

Would you please give me a ring and we can fix an appointment.

Yours sincerely,

(David Webster)
General Administrator.

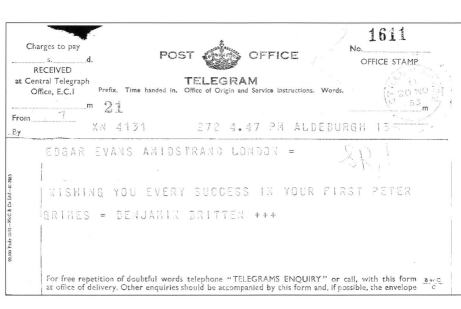

My dear Edgar,

Thank you very much indeed for your

good wishes for my birthday

✓ via telegram

Ben

Royal Opera House

COVENT GARDEN LONDON WC2

Telephone : Covent Garden 1200
Telegrams : Amidstrand

10th May, 1957.

My dear Edgar,

I want to thank you very much for your excellent spirit of co-operation and team-work, which you showed by stepping into "Turandot" at such short notice.

I especially appreciate your singing two performances in three nights, as I am well aware that this must have been a strain for you.

With all good wishes,

Yours sincerely,

Rafael Kubelik

Rafael Kubelik.

Royal Opera House

COVENT GARDEN LONDON WC2

27th August, 1963.

Telephone : Covent Garden 1200
Telegrams : Amidstrand

Edgar Evans, Esq.,

Dear Edgar,

    This is just to confirm that Sir David has agreed that you may go to Germany to work on "Lohengrin" with Dr. Hallasch, leaving on Thursday morning, and returning either for rehearsals on 17th or 23rd September.

    Sir David has agreed to keep you on your contractual salary during this period, to pay the cost of your return air fare to Munich and also to pay the cost of your tuition fees.

    Best wishes, and I hope all will go well,

                Yours sincerely,

VICTOR OLIVER

66 WESTMINSTER GARDENS

L O N D O N   S.W. I

TEL. VICTORIA 2640

22nd December, 1950.

Edgar Evans, Esq.,
Royal Opera House,
Covent Garden,
London, W.C.2.

Dear Edgar Evans,

I feel I must write and congratulate
you on your magnificent performance last
night.

I was tremendously impressed and
delighted by your success in this most
exacting role.

With kindest regards and wishing you
the Compliments of the Season,

I am,
Very sincerely yours,

Victor Oliver

ROYAL OPERA HOUSE

COVENT GARDEN

THURSDAY, 26th APRIL, 1951

THE ROYAL OPERA HOUSE, COVENT GARDEN LTD.

General Administrator: DAVID L. WEBSTER

presents

The first performance of

"THE PILGRIM'S PROGRESS"

A Morality in a Prologue, Four Acts and an Epilogue
founded on BUNYAN'S ALLEGORY of the same name

Music by

RALPH VAUGHAN WILLIAMS, O.M.

(by arrangement with the Oxford University Press)

Scenery and Costumes by Hal Burton

CONDUCTOR : LEONARD HANCOCK

PRODUCER : NEVILL COGHILL

Appendix Six: Nan Evans (nee Walters), 1910-1998

This tribute, written by Robert Little, was paid at
Nan Evans' funeral.

Time is short. Today, we have just 20 minutes to pay tribute to Nan, whose 88 years seem all too brief – crammed, as they were, with action.

It was some 20 years ago that I first met Nan. I was a hopeful and enthusiastic – rather than talented – singer, yet Nan would always find a word of encouragement for me, to spur me on to continue to develop what talent I had. She must have also thought that I needed feeding up, because she always offered me a cup of coffee and piece or two of home-made cake whenever I visited her home in Preston Hill, in Harrow.

Over the years, Nan continued to encourage not only me but also all the other singers who came to her husband, Edgar, for vocal training.

At times, Nan even ventured to offer some technical advice about the art of singing and voice production. Her knowledge of what was good vocal technique, she said, came from her many years of listening to, and being with, some of the best singers in the world – including, of course, Edgar. Not surprisingly, Nan was one of Edgar's greatest supporters. Up to the end of her life, she continued to campaign for further recognition of his many achievements in the operatic world.

Nan delighted in being part of the opera world, meeting and being greeted by the great and the good – including aristocracy and royalty.

The glittering lights of London's operatic society were a long and winding road away from the village of Lower Cwm Twrch, near Swansea, where Nan had been born.

Nan came to London soon enough – in her late teens – to take up a job as a children's nurse in Hampstead Garden Suburb. She had a number of employers, including the eminent heart specialist, Dr Shirley Smith, and the celebrated artist, Mark Gertler. This latter job took her to Spain from where she returned, along with the Gertlers, to escape the Spanish Civil War.

This association with painting resurfaced in later life, when Nan took up the brushes herself. She produced a number of pleasing paintings, demonstrating a great deal of artistic talent.

One of Nan's first actions on coming to London was to find – and join – the Welsh Congregational Church at King's Cross. It was there she met Edgar – a young singer, who had recently arrived in the city to join the Sadler's Wells Opera Company. After a two year engagement, they were married, on 19th August 1939 – just a fortnight before the outbreak of war.

Subsequently, for over 50 years, Nan devoted herself to caring for her own family – not only Edgar but also their son, Huw. Later, she became mother-in-law to Nicola and a devoted grandmother – to Rebecca and Edward.

Nan had three abiding passions: her large and wide-ranging family; her devotion to the community in which she lived, and the people and culture of her native Wales. Thankfully, Nan was often able to indulge these passions in combination.

Nan was able to transplant the Welsh love of 'community' to the foreign soil of Preston

● *Huw Evans.*

Hill and its environs. It was only recently that Nan had ceased to be a tenacious canvasser and tireless worker for the local Conservative party – helping the former Conservative government minister Rhodes Boyson, among others. But it was on an individual level that Nan's influence was most felt within the local community.

Nan knew a lot of people and a lot of people knew her. To all of these people, Nan offered a great deal of practical help willingly and tirelessly – and she continued to do this until the very last days of her long and fruitful life. She visited those who were ill; she babysat; she went shopping and did other jobs for those who were infirm, and – importantly – she was always there when people needed her. She listened, sympathised, consoled and encouraged.

In all that she did, Nan was motivated by a deep love of people. Love of others had called her from Wales all those years ago – to look after children. Love surfaced in a new and exciting way in that Welsh Congregational Chapel at King's Cross – and opened up for Nan a long and successful career as a wife and mother. It prompted her to be active within the communities with which she was associated. It was nurtured by her Christian faith and encapsulated in a small book, which Nan always carried with her in her handbag: a commentary on

● *Nan, with Edgar, relaxing at their home in Harrow.*

chapter 13 of Paul's first letter to the Corinthians and called 'The Greatest Thing in the World'.

Nan did a great many things in her long life – except one. Despite the many demands made on her time and energy by others, she never complained. She never even complained when the pain of her last illness had sapped both her energy and her seemingly boundless good humour. Ask her how she was and the answer was always the same: 'not too bad'.

Although she had not lived in Wales for over 60 years, Nan never lost her Welsh accent nor her love of all things Welsh. In her kitchen, proudly displayed on the wall, is a plaque which reads: 'To be born Welsh is to be born privileged. Not with a silver spoon in your mouth, but music in your blood and poetry in your soul.'

Nan's life took her into the world of professional music. She took to it well, because music was in her blood. She expressed the poetry in her soul in practical ways: in loving service to others – her family and her many friends.

It is we – who have known her and whose lives she has enriched – who are privileged.

List of illustrations

Edgar Evans 5

At a party in Bulawayo with, among others, Joan Sutherland and Geraint Evans (*photo Janet Chivers*) 7

Cwrt Farm, with Edgar's sister Maggie and brother Dai 11

Edgar's mother, Margaret, making butter 12

Scenes of Cwrt Newydd before the First World War 15

On holiday in Newquay, Cardiganshire: Edgar (aged four) with his parents and brother Will 16

Newquay School teachers and pupils, 1929 18

Luigi Ricci and his son 28

Lawrance Collingwood 33

Geoffrey Corbett 34

With Esther Salaman in the Ephesian Matron 39

On tour to Ireland, 1942, with, among others, Joyce Grenfell and Richard Addinsell (*photo Belfast Telegraph*) (*Picture reproduced with kind permission of Belfast Telegraph Newspapers Ltd*) 41

Opera for All in Bridgewater, with Edgar as Basilio in the Marriage of Figaro 44

Henry Robinson 46

Edgar in the Anglo-Russian Merry Go Round (*photo Jean Straker*) 47

As Dmitri in Boris Godunov, with Constance Shacklock as Marina (*photo Angus McBean*) 53

Edgar and Nan's son, Huw 55

As Calaf in Turandot (*photo Derek Allen*) 56

On horseback in The Tatler, 1959 57

David Niven's horse meets the cast of Boris Godunov at Covent Garden (*photo Daily Herald*) (*Picture reproduced with kind permission of Science & Society Picture Library*) 58

Arriving in Wiesbaden 62

Rehearsing with Benjamin Britten and Tyrone Guthrie, while Peter Gellhorn is on the telephone 63

Edgar as Bob Boles (*photo Houston Rogers*) 63

Rehearsing with Victoria de los Angeles. Warwick Brithwaite is the conductor, with Monia Young at the piano (*photo Mirrorpic*) (*Picture reproduced with kind permission of Mirrorpix*) 67

Edgar as Zinovy in Katerina Ismailova (*photo Houston Rogers*) 69

Carlo Maria Giulini 70

Edgar as Count Lerma in Don

Carlos   (*photo Houston Rogers*)
70

Rehearsing Pilgrim's Progress
with Ralph Vaughan Williams
(*photo Charles H Hewitt, Picture
Post*)   71

With Vaughan Williams, Adele
Leigh and Iris Kells (*photo Charles
H Hewitt, Picture Post*)   71

At the end of A Masked Ball with
Jess Walters, Adele Leigh and
Helena Verte (*photo Denis de
Marney*)   72

Edgar as Melot in Tristan und
Isolde (*photo Houston Rogers*)   73

Edgar as Riccardo in A Masked
Ball (*photo Denis de Marney*)   75

Edgar's first car – a Railton drop
head coupe, one of only 24 ever
made   76

Georg Solti with Dr Hallasch   77

Edgar is presented to the Queen
on the Royal Opera House's 21st
anniversary. In the background is
John Tooley (*photo Reg Wilson*)   79

With Lord Harewood (*photo
Barratt's*)   80

Edgar, as Count Lerma (in Don
Carlos) meets the Queen Mother
at Covent Garden (*photo Reg
Wilson*)   81

Edgar as Dmitri in Boris Godunov
(*photo Angus McBean*)   83

Edgar as the Drum Major in
Wozzeck (*photo Houston Rogers*)   85

Edgar, in his debut role of des
Grieux in Manon (photo Edward
Mandinian), Pinkerton in Madam
Butterfly, Mx in Der Freischutz
and Riccardo in A Masked Ball
(*photos Denis de Marney*)   90

At home with his wife, Nan, during his enforced absence from
Covent Garden (*photo Northcliffe
Newspapers Group) (Picture
reproduced with kind permission
of Associated Newspapers*)   91

Making up as Hermann in the
Queen of Spades (photo Mirrorpic)
(*Picture reproduced with kind
permission of Mirrorpix*)   94

With Edith Coates (the Countess)
in the Queen of Spades (*photo
Barratt's*)   97

Edgar as Hermann in the Queen
of Spades (*photo Angus McBean*)
99

About to get some broken ribs in
Carmen (*photo Roger Wood*)   103

With Helena Verte in A Masked
Ball (*photo Denis de Marney*)   106

The aspiring opera singer and the
accomplished teacher (photo
Donald Southern); signing autographs, and off to sing in Toulouse
– saying farewell to his son, Huw,
and wife, Nan (*photo Barratt's*) 111

Edgar, with Elsie Morrison, in
Arwel Hughes' opera, Menna   117

Edgar as Captain Davidson in
Victory (*photo Dominic*)   118

Edgar as Pang in Turandot *(photo Baron)*   124

Edgar as Vogelgesang in The Mastersingers *(photo Houston Rogers)*   124

Edgar, as Don Jose, with Constance Shacklock as Carmen *(photo Roger Wood)*   152

Letter from Lilian Bayliss, at Sadler's Wells Opera, 27th May 1937   153

Edgar Evans' discharge from the Metropolitan Police, 24th June 1942   154

Letter from Wembley Police Garage Athletic Club, 5th June 1950   154

Letters from the Royal Opera House, 8th April 1946 and 31st July 1946   156

Letter to Edgar Evans from David Webster, 14th August 1946   157

Telegrams to Edgar Evans from David Webster and Benjamin Britten   158

Note to Edgar Evans from Benjamin Britten   159

Letter to Edgar Evans from Rafael Kubelick, 10th May 1957   159

Letter from the Royal Opera House, 27th August 1963   160

Letter from Vic Oliver   161

Cover of the programme for the first performance of Vaughan Williams' 'The Pilgrim's Progress', signed by the composer   162

Huw Evans   164

Edgar and Nan at home in Harrow *(photo Northcliffe Newspapers Group) (Picture reproduced with kind permission of Associated Newspapers)*   165

We have made extensive enquiries to find the photographers and copyright holders for these photographs but have had limited success. Nonetheless, we would like to acknowledge the help given to us by the National Portrait Gallery, the National Museum of Photography, Film and Television, the Theatre Museum Collection and the Victoria & Albert Museum.

Index

Aberystwyth 13, 14
Aberystwyth, University College 9
Ackland, Essie 122
Addinsell, Richard 3, 41
Adey, Frank 45, 47
Ainley, Richard 26
Alan, Harvey 109
Aldeburgh 60, 137
Aldridge, Herbert 120
Allister, Jean 142
Alltgoch Farm 79, 80
Amis, John 138, 139
Amsterdam 106
Anders, Peter 54
Anderson, Andy 85, 86, 106
Anthony, Cyril 130
Anthony, Trevor 126
Arnold, Malcolm 138, 139
Arts Council 38, 47
Ashby, Jonathan 138, 139
Ashton, Frederick 35
Askey, Arthur 109
Austin, Sumner 84
Austral, Florence 120
Ayling, Joan 69
Baillie, Isobel 65, 123
Baines, Francis 138, 139
Bainton, John 141
Balestrieri, John 20
Balfour, Margaret 120
Barber, Nancy 19
Barbirolli, John 4, 5, 6, 49, 76, 102, 119, 130, 131, 132, 133
Barbone, Nina 44, 113, 128
Barker, Daphne 109
Barker, Eric 110, 135
Barker, Jack 109
Basted, Ted 33, 93
Baylis, Lillian 3, 32, 33, 34, 153
BBC 83, 84, 109, 128, 135, 136, 137, 140, 142
Bean, Ernest 138, 139
Beecham, Thomas 5, 35, 49, 66, 67, 146
Bel, Pierre 110, 135
Belcher, Cecil 28

Berenska, Jan 120
Berg, Alban 84, 98
Berisova, Svetlana 109
Berkeley, Lennox 39
Berlin State Opera 93, 99, 101
Birkett, Mr 30, 31
Blackburn, Harold 60
Blacker, Thetis 139
Bliss, Arthur 65
Boosey & Hawkes Ltd 144
Bowman, Audrey 106
Boyson, Rhodes 165
Braden, Bernard 109
Brain, Dennis 110, 135
Braithwaite, Warwick 19, 127, 129
Brannigan, Owen 65, 123, 138, 139
Britten, Benjamin 5, 56, 57, 60, 62, 63, 69, 89, 158, 159
Brook, Peter 1, 57, 59, 114, 146
Brouwenstijn, Gré 4, 75
Brown, Mamie 120
Brown, May 129
Bulawayo 6, 7, 133, 147
Butler, Joan 125
Callaghan, Domini 109
Callas, Maria 57, 100
Camberwell 2, 30
Cameron, John 134
Cantelo, April 138, 139
Carl Rosa Opera 108
Carroll, Christina 126
Carron, Arthur 4, 55
Caruso, Enrico 2, 4, 16, 19, 73, 101
Catley, Gwen 56
Cave, Alfred 1
CEMA 3, 38, 39, 40, 41, 43, 44
Charing Cross Hospital 104
Christoff, Boris 57, 58, 75, 83, 100, 110
Choral Symphony, Beethoven 4
Clapham 14, 25, 32
Clifford, Graham 49, 122
Coates, Edith 8, 27, 36, 102, 125, 126, 135, 138, 139
Coco the Clown 109
Coghill, Nevill 162

Coleman, Arthur 122
Collingwood, Lawranceœ 33, 34
Collins, Bessie 126
Cooper, Joseph 128, 138
Copland, Aaron 138
Copp, Ruby 27
Corbett, Geoffrey 3, 33, 34, 38, 40, 122
Corlett, Gladys 120
County Architects' Office, Llandysul 20, 21
Cox, John 6
Cresswell, Zoe 127
Cross, Joan 28, 61
Crowfoot, Alan 117
Crute, Francis 120
Cwrt Farm 11, 13, 14, 16, 23, 47, 92
Cwrt Newydd, Cardiganshire 2, 11, 14, 17, 20, 24, 47
Cymanfa Ganu 11
Dalberg, Frederick 99, 106
Dali, Salvador 1
Daniels, Bebe 12
Daniels, Idris 26
Dargavel, Bruce 34, 36, 38, 123, 125, 130, 132, 134, 136
Davidson, Gladys 48, 69, 74
Davies 135
Davies, David 45
Davies, Gerald 83, 151
Davies, Goronwy (Gonny) 14
Davies, Jennie 136
Davies, Lawton 26
Davies, Meredith 60, 140
Davies, Mollie 126
Davies, Mr (headmaster of Cwrt Newydd school) 14, 17
Davies, Murray 119
Davies, Rhydderch 74, 101, 104
Day, Frances 110, 135
de Gunst, Molly 36
Delfont, Bernard 3, 45, 113
Delman, Jacqueline 137, 138
del Mar, Norman 107, 138, 139
de los Angeles, Victoria 67, 68
Denise, Gita 128
de Reske, Jean 4, 73
Desti, Roberta 141

Diaghilev, Sergei 35
Dibdin, Charles 39
Dickie, Murray 66
Dickie, William 66
Dobrowen, Issay 132
Dobson, John 138, 139
Domingo, Placido 8
Donlevy 135
Dowd, Ronald 53, 54
Downes, Edward (Ted) 88, 135, 136, 141, 142
Dwyryd, Telynores/Eleanor 130, 141
Easton, Robert 65, 121
Edwards, Lesley 35
Edgware 42
Eisteddfod/au 2, 14, 19, 20
Elijah 65, 120
Elliott, Victoria 129, 133
Ellis, Osian 140
English National Opera 80
ENSA 3, 38, 39, 43, 44, 47
Etherington, James (Jimmy) 45
Evans, Brenda 88
Evans, David (Dai) (brother) 13, 14, 20, 22, 23, 25, 26, 30, 32, 33
Evans, David (nephew) 32
Evans, David (no relation) 79, 80
Evans, Edith 138, 139
Evans, Elizabeth (sister) 14
Evans, Evan (brother) 13
Evans, Geraint 51, 79, 84, 85, 86, 87, 88
Evans, Hannah (sister) 13, 14, 23
Evans, Huw (son) 5, 33, 41, 47, 55, 76, 104, 164
Evans, John (Jack) (brother) 13
Evans, Prof Dr Leonard (nephew 13
Evans, Margaret (mother) 1, 2, 12, 14, 33
Evans, Margaret (Maggie) (sister) 14
Evans, Margaret 121
Evans (nee Walters), Nan (wife) 5, 9, 26, 37, 38, 47, 76, 85, 89, 104, 163, 164
Evans, Nicola (daughter-in-law) 164
Evans, Rachel (sister) 14
Evans, Samuel (brother) 13
Evans, Sarah (sister) 14
Evans, Simon (brother) 13, 18, 23

Evans, Vernon (Vernie) (brother)   13
Evans, William (father) 1, 2, 12, 16, 23
Evans, William (brother)   13, 18, 22, 23
Fagg, Arthur   2, 25, 26
Feasey, Norman 54
Ferrier, Kathleen   65, 121, 123
Finneberg, Laelia   126
Fischer-Dieskau, Dietrich   73
Fisher, Sylvia   61, 106, 131, 135
Flagstadt, Kirsten   73
Fonteyn, Margot   3, 34, 35
Ford's of Dagenham   18
Fox's (theatrical costumiers), London 45,
46
Foy, Patricia   137
Fear, Arthur   108
Franklin, David   83, 84
Freer, Dawson   2, 26, 27, 28, 29, 40
Free Wales Army   79
French, Leslie   133
Furtwangler, Wilhelm   5, 73
Galliver, David   138
Gardner, John   8, 73
Gardiner, John   92
Garrard, Don   117
Garrick Club   94
Gellhorn, Peter 5, 66, 92, 93, 95, 96, 98,
130
George, Norman   141
Geraldo (Gerald Bright)   33
Gertler, Mark   26, 164
Ghiourov, Nicolai   58
Gill, Henry   120
Gipps, Bryan   120
Glendinning, Reginald   129
Glossop, Peter   109, 138, 139
Glyndebourne   4, 6, 40, 142
Glynne, Walter   40
Glynne, Howell   59, 114, 127, 133, 135
Gielgud, John   140
Gigli, Beniamino   33, 93
Gilbert & Sullivan   10, 78, 152
Giulini, Carlo Maria   5, 49, 70, 138
Gobbi, Tito   4, 72, 73
Godfrey, Brian   57, 107
Gomer Lewis, Ethel   123
Goodall, Reginald   3, 60, 88, 89, 123,
127, 133, 135, 138, 141, 142
Goodwright, Peter   141
Gough Matthews, Michael   9
Graham, Colin   138, 139
Grand Theatre, Leeds   81
Green, Joseph   65
Grenfell, Joyce   3, 41, 81
Griffiths, David (Dai)   23
Griffiths, Mervyn   121
Griffiths, Netta   130
Griffiths, Vernon   13, 14, 23, 79
Gundry, Inglis   39
Guthrie, Tyrone   106, 135
Hague, The   106
Hallasch, Dr   77, 160
Halle Orchestra   102, 131
Hambourg   77
Hamburger, Paul   39
Hammond-Stroud, Derek   117
Hampstead   27, 37, 38, 41, 164
Hancock, Leonard   129, 162
Hannesson, Thorsteinn   2, 53
Harding, Mrs   19
Harewood, Lord   80, 81
Harper Adams College   13
Harper, Heather   140
Harry, Lyn   127
Hawes, Elizabeth   133
Hemming, Percy   93
Henderson (bass)   44
Her Majesty, Queen Elizabeth   58, 78
Her Royal Highness, Princess Diana 78
Her Royal Highness, Princess Margaret
80
Hetty, the hen   102
Hill, Benny   119, 134
Hill, Martin   108
Hill, Rose   139
Hislop, Joseph (Joe)   74
His Royal Highness, Prince Charles 78,
80
Hitler, Adolf   107
Hoffnung, Gerard   138, 139
Hoffnung Interplanetary Festival   58,
107, 138, 139
Holdom, Gordon   126
Holmes, John   142

Horace (dresser) 101
Hordern, Michael 3, 48
Horne, Kenneth 119, 128
Horne, Marilyn 105
Horovitz, Joseph 138, 139
Howard, Patricia Martina 129
Howard, Trevor 109
Howells, John 110
Howell-Wilson, Grace 132
Hughes, Arwel 140
Hugheson, E H 142
Hunter, Ian 138, 139
Hurrey, Leslie 146
Hutton, Leonard (Len) 102
Ibbs & Tillett 64, 65
Ina (girlfriend) 24, 25
Ingpen, Joan 66
Irish House, The, Piccadilly 2, 25, 26
Isabelle (accompanist) 19
Iskoldoff, Eugene 112
Ivor (postman) 47
Jacopi 135
Jarred, Mary 125
Jenkin, Peter 108
Jenkins, WHJ 125
Jobin, Raoul 94, 97
Johnson, Margaret 109
Johnston, James (Jimmy) 52, 53, 55, 56, 66, 80, 82, 83, 89, 104, 143
Jones, David Lloyd 5
Jones, Delme Bryn 109
Jones, Dora 17, 18
Jones, Mary 136
Jones, Morgan 129
Jones, Mr (headmaster of Newquay School) 17
Jones, Myra 121
Jones, Rhys FRIBA 20
Kamargue, Jane 40
Kate, the horse 58
Kelly, Barbara 109
Kempe, Rudolfe 5, 49, 133, 136, 140
Kendall, Mary 140
Kerran, David – see Trevor, Harry (Clifford) 41, 42
Keynes, Lord 144
Kleiber, Erich 1, 4, 5, 49, 70, 75, 76, 84, 85, 87, 88, 93, 94, 95, 96, 97, 98, 100, 101, 106, 107, 108, 128, 130, 131, 132, 146
Klemperer, Otto 5, 49
Konwitschny, Franz 139
Kubelik, Rafael 1, 5, 136, 137, 145, 159
Krause, Clemens 5
Krause, Otakar 85, 98, 106, 135, 138, 139
Krombholc, Jaroslav 139
Kucharek, Helen 10
La Scala, Milan 40, 98, 100
Lambert, Constant 119, 123, 145
Lane, Gloria 138
Lane, Margaret 57
Langdon, Michael 88, 139
Lanigan 135
Le Brun, Monsieur, President of France 35
Legge, Walter 3, 73
Leon (dresser) 101, 104
Leonard, Lawrence 138, 139
Lester, Bert 120
Lewis, the Rev Elfed 26
Lewis, Idris 119
Lewis, Richard 59, 62, 64, 82, 83, 114
Lewis, Ron 88
Liverpool 93, 147
Liverpool Philharmonic Society 145
Llandysul County School 17
Llanfyllyn 13
Llanybydder 14, 23, 47
Llewellyn, Redvers 9, 36, 109
Lloyd George, David 26
Lloyd, Harry 27
London Choral Society, The 2, 25
London Philharmonic Orchestra 102
Los Angeles Guild Opera 105
Lyon, Ben 112
Lyons Corner House 26
Maher, Patrick 129
Major, John 2
MacDonald, Ken 85
Mackerras, Charles 39, 137
Macmillan, Hamish 103, 104
Marno, Dorothy 134
Mason, Stanley 128

Matheson, John 140
McBain, David 138, 139
McCracken, James 8
McWalters, Virginia 93
Melville, George 129
Messel, Oliver 146
Messiah, The 64, 65, 113, 118, 121, 123, 130, 142
Metropolitan Opera, New York 55
Midgeley, Walter 66, 89, 113, 143
Millar, Mary 134
Mills 135
Mitchell, Ena 130
Mitchell, Eric 92, 94, 95
Morgan, Edward 121
Morgan, Gerwyn 141
Morgan-Lewis, Decima 134
Motor Show, The, Earls' Court, London 106
Munich 77, 160
Murdoch, Richard 119, 128
My Music, BBC radio programme 83
Nash, Heddle 3, 48, 89
Nash, Stuart 41
National & Provincial Bank 18
Neate, Kenneth 47
Neher, Caspar 146
Nevern, Grace 119
Newcastle Emlyn 13
Newquay School 2, 17, 19, 20, 21
Nightingales 62
Nilsson, Raymond 53, 54, 62, 135, 143
Niblette, Lillian 120
Niven, David 58
Noble, Dennis 89, 138
Noble, John 60
Northern Ireland 41, 82
Nowakowski, Marian 59, 73, 107, 123, 130, 134
Odd Spot, The 2, 25, 26
O'Donnell, Josephine 46, 155, 156
Oliver, Vic 109, 110, 137, 161

Operas
Aida 36, 66, 107, 138, 143
Albert Herring 5, 57, 60
Barber of Seville, The 152
Bartered Bride, The 105
Beggar's Opera, The 122, 144
Billy Budd 5, 61, 69, 79, 115, 116, 130, 142, 147
Blodwen 129
Bohemian Girl, The 146
Boris Godunov 1, 5, 52, 53, 57, 58, 59, 69, 83, 102, 103, 108, 110, 114, 125, 127, 132, 139, 141, 146
Carmellites, The 143
Carmen 3, 4, 8, 46, 49, 52, 53, 56, 57, 69, 81, 88, 89, 101, 103, 104, 108, 117, 119, 134, 135, 143, 145, 146
Cavalleria Rusticana 34, 36, 69
Der Ring Des Nibelungen / Das Rheingold 1, 4, 98, 106, 128, 131, 136, 139, 140, 143, 146
Der Freischutz 4, 89, 135, 136
Don Carlos 5, 70, 83, 138
Elektra 1, 132, 143, 146
Ephesian Matron, The 39, 40, 122
Faerie Queen, The 3, 28, 48, 118, 119, 123, 145
Faithful Sentinel, The 122
Falstaff 119
Fidelio 69
Flying Dutchman, The 52, 69, 128
Girl of the Golden West, The 46
Gotterdammerung 143
Jenufa 1, 5, 137
Katerina Ismailova 1, 69, 141
La Boheme 6, 7, 47, 69, 122, 132, 133, 143
La Favorita 29
La Gioconda 107
Lohengrin 77
Madam Butterfly 4, 89, 135, 143
Magic Flute, The 46, 87, 88, 93, 143, 146
Manon 3, 48, 67, 68, 69, 89, 92, 93, 113, 114, 123, 129
Marriage of Figaro, The 47, 122, 143
Masked Ball, A 1, 4, 69, 72, 73, 75, 89, 105, 116, 131, 133, 143
Mastersingers, The 53, 54, 66, 67, 84, 124, 138, 142, 146
Mazeppa 59
Norma 146

Olympians, The 138
Otello 55, 143, 146
Parsifal 142, 146
Partisans, The 39
Peter Grimes 4, 60, 61, 62, 63, 89, 116, 133, 135, 140, 143, 147, 158
Pilgrim's Progress 1, 70, 115, 129, 162
Policeman's Serenade, The 122
Queen of Spades, The 1, 5, 52, 69, 70, 74, 87, 93, 94, 95, 97, 98, 108, 115, 128, 129, 136, 146
Rake's Progress, The 6
Rigoletto 8, 9, 143
Rosenkavalier, Der 93, 95, 96, 114, 124, 146
Ruth 39, 137
Salome 1, 69, 107, 108, 110, 127, 128, 133, 136, 138, 140
Sicilian Vespers, The 57, 100
Tales of Hoffmann, The 66, 89, 116, 136, 143, 146
Tosca 3, 46, 143
Traviata, La 69, 73, 106, 127
Tristan und Isolde 5, 73, 124, 146
Trojans, The 1, 140, 143
Trovatore, Il 54, 55, 77, 109, 137, 143
Turandot 4, 5, 56, 57, 69, 76, 89, 110, 115, 123, 130, 134, 137, 143, 146, 159
Valkyrie, The 87, 143
Victory 1, 119, 142
Visit of the Old Lady, The 4, 6, 117, 142
Wozzeck 1, 5, 69, 84, 85, 86, 87, 98, 100, 105, 108, 117, 130, 132, 135, 142, 146
Opera for All 44
Opera Sempre 109
Palace Theatre, The, London 45
Paris 3, 61, 147
Patzak, Julius 116
Pavarotti, Luciano 8
Pavilion Opera 10
Payne, Lawrence 110
Pearce, Judith 139
Pears, Peter 5, 27, 39, 60, 61, 62, 63, 115, 116, 143
Peters, Captain (P&O Line) 20
Peters, Ina 20
Picaver, Alfred 75

Police 3, 37, 38, 42, 154
Pollack, Louis 120
Pollard, Shackleton 56
Popplewell, Richard 9
Poston, Elizabeth 138, 139
Pritchard, John 6, 75, 88, 131, 133, 134, 135, 142

Productions
Anglo-Russian Merry Go Round, The 3, 44, 47, 112
Gay Review, The 45, 113
Gay Rosalinda 3, 45, 64
Salome: Brook-Dali 1
Puttnam, Jack L 134
Rae, Muriel 121
Railton, drop-head coupe 76
Randell, Sheila 133
Rankl, Karl 5, 46, 49, 50, 52, 57, 84, 93, 107, 124, 125, 127, 128, 129, 145, 156
Rawlings, Margaret 126
Reece, Brian 110, 135
Rees, Sam 18
Reilly, Tommy 141
Rennert, Gunther 105, 106
Requiem, Verdi 65
Ricci, Luigi 2, 4, 28, 72, 73, 75, 76
Rich, John 144
Richards-Thomas, Winnie 122
Rix, Sheila 138, 139
Roberton, Dorothy 129
Robertson, Duncan 138, 139
Robey, George 36
Robinson, Douglas 8
Robinson, Forbes 77
Robinson, Henry 3, 36, 45, 46
Roles:
Aegisth, Elektra 1, 132, 143
Alberich, The Ring 106
Alfred, Gay Rosalinda 45
Alfredo, La Traviata 69, 73
Amelia, A Masked Ball ...116
Andres, Wozzeck 1, 69, 84, 98, 130, 132
Armand, La Traviata 127
Bacchus, The Olympians 65, 138
Basilio, The Marriage of Figaro 122
Billy Budd, Billy Budd 61
Boaz, Ruth 39, 40, 137

Bob Boles, Peter Grimes 62, 140
Boris, Boris Godunov 83
Borza, Rigoletto 8
Butler, The, The Visit of the Old Lady 4, 117, 142
Calaf, Turandot 4, 5, 27, 56, 57, 69, 76, 89, 115, 130, 134, 137
Captain Davidson, Victory 1, 142
Captain Vere, Billy Budd 5, 61, 69, 79, 115, 116, 130, 142
Carmen, Carmen 81, 108
Centurion, The Ephesian Matron 122
Chevalier des Grieux, The, Manon 3, 4, 48, 67, 69, 89, 92, 114, 123, 129
Dancairo, El, Carmen 49, 52
David, The Mastersingers 67
Dmitri, The Pretender, Boris Godunov 1, 5, 52, 53, 58, 69, 83, 102, 108, 125, 127, 132, 139, 141
Don Jose, Carmen 4, 8, 52, 53, 56, 57, 69, 88, 89, 103, 104, 105, 108, 117, 119, 134, 135, 143
Drum Major, The, Wozzeck 5, 84, 85, 86, 87, 98, 105, 117, 135, 142
Duke, The, Rigoletto 8
Eisenstein, Gay Rosalinda 45
Ellen Orford, Peter Grimes 61
Erik, The Flying Dutchman 52, 69, 128
Escamillo, Carmen 88, 89, 103
Filch, The Beggar's Opera 122
First Knight, The, Parsifal 142
First Man in Armour, The Magic Flute 87
Florestan, Fidelio 69
Froh, Das Rheingold 1, 98, 114, 128, 131, 136, 139, 140
God of the Birds & A Lover, The Faerie Queen 3, 48, 123
Hata, The Bartered Bride 105
Hellenus, The Trojans 1, 140
Henry, The Faithful Sentinel 122
Hermann, The Queen of Spades 1, 5, 52, 69, 70, 74, 87, 93, 94, 95, 97, 98, 108, 115, 128, 129, 136
Hoffmann, The Tales of Hoffmann 66, 89, 116, 136
Hostess, Boris Godunov 103

Interpreter, The, & A Celestial Messenger, Pilgrim's Progress 1, 70, 115, 129
Italian tenor, Der Rosenkavalier 124
John the Baptist, Salome 107
King of Egypt, The, Aida 107
Landlord, Der Rosenkavalier 124
Lerma, Don Carlos 5, 70, 72, 138
Lohengrin, Lohengrin 77, 160
Luna, Il Trovatore 109
Manon, Manon 93
Manrico, Il Trovatore 54, 55, 109, 137
Marie, Wozzeck 105
Marina, Boris Godunov 102
Marschallin, Der Rosenkavalier 114
Max, Der Freischutz 4, 89, 135, 136
Mayor, The, Albert Herring 57, 60
Melot, Tristan und Isolde 5, 73
Milkman, The, The Policeman's Serenade 122
Moser, The Mastersingers 142
Narraboth, Salome 1, 69, 110, 127, 128, 133, 136, 138, 140
Nightwatchman, The Mastersingers 84
Ochs, Der Rosenkavalier 114
Octavian, Der Rosenkavalier 114
Otello, Otello 55
Pang, Turandot 123
Peter Grimes, Peter Grimes 4, 5, 60, 61, 62, 63, 89, 116, 133, 158
Philip of Spain, Don Carlos 83
Pimen, Boris Godunov 83
Pinkerton, Madam Butterfly 4, 89, 135
Radames, Aida 107, 138
Radcliffe, Mr, Billy Budd 61
Rake, The, The Rake's Progress 6
Redburn, Mr, Billy Budd 61
Renato, A Masked Ball 75
Riccardo (Gustavus), A Masked Ball 1, 69, 73, 75, 89, 105, 116, 131, 133
Roman Centurion, The Ephesian Matron 39
Rudolfo, La Boheme 6, 7, 69, 122, 132, 133, 158
Second Man in Armour, The Magic Flute 87
Sieglinde, The Ring 106

Sir Hywel Ddu, Blodwen   129
Smuggler, Carmen   104
Steersman, The Flying Dutchman   128
Steva, Jenufa   1, 5, 137
Turiddu, Cavalleria Rusticana   69
Vogelgesang, The Mastersingers   53, 67, 124
Walther, The Mastersingers   53, 54, 138
Wozzeck, Wozzeck   84
Young Seaman, Tristan und Isolde   124
Zinovy, Katerina Ismailova   1, 69, 141
Zuniga, Carmen   101, 104
Rome   4, 56, 76, 86, 98, 106
Rome Opera   56, 98, 99, 106, 131
Rothmuller, Marco   84
Rowlands, Ceinwen   121
Royal Albert Hall, The   65, 118, 131
Royal Arsenal Co-Operative Society, The   2, 30, 31
Royal College of Music, The   2, 5, 9, 10, 26, 29, 31, 40, 41, 42, 66, 78
Royal Festival Hall   107, 138, 139
Royal Garden Party, Buckingham Palace   9
Royal Opera, Covent Garden   1, 2, 3, 4, 5, 6, 7, 9, 16, 24, 28, 31, 35, 36, 38, 42, 44, 45, 46, 47, 48, 49, 51, 52, 53, 54, 55, 56, 58, 60, 61, 62, 67, 68, 69, 70, 73, 74, 75, 76, 77, 78, 79, 80, 82, 83, 84, 86, 87, 88, 89, 92, 93, 96, 97, 98, 100, 101, 102, 103, 104, 105, 107, 109, 110, 113, 116, 117, 122, 124, 125, 127, 128, 129, 130, 131, 132, 133, 134, 135, 136, 137, 138, 139, 140, 141, 142, 143, 144, 145, 155, 156, 157, 159, 160, 162
Rugby   football   2, 25, 87
Ryde, Isle of Wight   3, 45, 46, 113
Sadler's Wells Ballet   34, 35, 145
Sadler's Wells Opera Company, The   3, 9, 24, 27, 28, 29, 32, 33, 34, 36, 37, 38, 45, 46, 54, 55, 83, 105, 108, 109, 153, 164
Salaman, Esther   39, 120
Sale, Frank   51, 52
Sales, Freddie   110, 135
San Francisco Opera   105
Sargent, Malcolm 5, 49, 64, 65, 66, 113, 123, 138
Schiller, Allan   134
Schramm, Herr   61, 62
Schwarzkopf, Elizabeth   51, 73
Searle, Humphrey   138, 139
Seasons, The   64
Seiber, Matyas   138, 139
Seymour, Tommy   120
Shacklock, Constance 3, 39, 59, 81, 92, 94, 98, 102, 106, 108, 110, 114, 129, 131
Shaw, John   61
Shearer, Moira   3
Shirley Smith, Dr   38, 164
Shostakovich, Dmitry   69
Shuard, Amy   109, 137
Silveri, Paulo   58
Sinclair, Monica   60
Sladen, Victoria   24, 131
Slater, Lionel   138, 139
Sleeping Princess, The (ballet)   35
Slobotskyia, Oda   5
Smith, Fabian   44
Solti, Georg   5, 49, 61, 77, 142
Southern Rhodesia   6
Spanish Civil War   164
Stephenson, Dennis   47, 48
Strauss, Richard   107
Studholme, Marion   142
Sulikowski, J   134
Sumner, Barbara   128
Susskind, Walter   129, 131
Sutherland, Joan   75, 116
Swift, Frank   104
Tangye, Hilary   108
Tatham, Miss   38
Tauber, Richard   3, 45
Tausky, Vilem   129, 134
Teatro Colon, Buenos Aires, Argentina   55, 101, 107
Te Wiata, Inia   141
Television   56, 109, 137, 140
Terry, Patrick   49, 50
Terry-Thomas   109
Teyte, Maggie   3
Thomas, D Francgon   140
Thomas, Frank   120
Thomas, Mansel   119

Thomas, Nancy 137
Thompson, Eric 138, 139
Titterton, Frank 27, 33, 93
Todds, Walter 139
Tooley, John 9
Towyn Chapel, Newquay 20
Trevor, Harry (Clifford) – see Kerran,
David 41, 42
Trevor, John 41
Turner, Blanche 8, 123, 125, 126, 130,
135, 143
Turner, Harold 35
Unitarian chapel 17, 19
University of Buckingham 13
Upman, Theodore 61
Valevska, Zoya 112
Vaughan, Elizabeth 141
Vaughan Williams, Ralph 70, 115, 162
Verte, Helena 75
Vickers, Jon 8, 62, 63, 143
Vienna 75
Vienna State Opera 67
Visconti, Luchino 70, 72
Vyvyan, Jennifer 130
Wakhevitch, Georges 146
Walker, Nina 139
Walker, Norman 107, 131
Wallace, Ian 138, 139
Walters, Edgar (brother-in-law) 26
Walters, Jess 64, 66, 75, 84, 106, 138
Waterford, the horse 58

Watts, Helen 140
Webster, David 3, 38, 47, 50, 53, 54, 62,
70, 76, 80, 81, 86, 88, 89, 93, 94, 97, 98,
100, 106, 145, 157, 158, 160
Weldon, George 131
Welsh College of Music and Drama 83
Welsh Revival (1904) 12
Welwyn Opera 39
West, Christopher 88, 146
White, Cecil 122
White, Leyland 129
Whitland, Cardiganshire 14
Whitlock, Percy 121
Widdup, Walter 27
Wiesbaden 61, 62, 135, 147
Wigmore Studios 27
Wilbur, Jay 112
Willcocks, David 5, 9
Williams, Len 108
Williams, Maimie 130
Williams, Meirion 126, 130, 134
Williams, Tom 8, 125, 126
Wilson, Kepple and Betty 45
Wilson, Steuart 38, 94, 98
Wimbourne, Lord 14
Winston, the horse 57, 58
Worden, Wilfred 126
Wright, John (Jack) 36
Wtorzecka, Janina 134
Young, Emanuel 135
Ystradgynlais 58, 130